ESSAYS IN INTERNATIONAL ECONOMICS

No. 219, September 2000

G-3 EXCHANGE-RATE RELATIONSHIPS: A REVIEW OF THE RECORD AND OF PROPOSALS FOR CHANGE

RICHARD H. CLARIDA

INTERNATIONAL ECONOMICS SECTION

DEPARTMENT OF ECONOMICS
PRINCETON UNIVERSITY
PRINCETON, NEW JERSEY

INTERNATIONAL ECONOMICS SECTION
EDITORIAL STAFF

Library of Congress Cataloging-in-Publication Data

Clarida, Richard H.
   G-3 exchange-rate relationships: a review of the record and of proposals for change / Richard H. Clarida.
      p. cm. — (Essays in international economics, ISSN 0071-142X ; no. 219)
   Includes bibliographical references.
   ISBN 0-88165-126-5
   1. Foreign exchange rates. I. Title: G-3 exchange-rate relationships. II. Princeton University. International Economics Section. III. Title. IV. Essays in International economics (Princeton, N.J.); no. 219

HG136.P7 no. 219
[HG3851]
332'.042 s   00-058066
[332.4'5 21]   CIP
JK

Printed in the United States of America by Princeton University Printing Services at Princeton, New Jersey

International Standard Serial Number: 0071-142X
International Standard Book Number: 0-88165-126-5
Library of Congress Catalog Card Number: 00-058066

International Economics Section
   Department of Economics, Fisher Hall
   Princeton University
   Princeton, New Jersey 08544-1021

Tel: 609-258-4048
Fax: 609-258-1374
E-mail: ies@princeton.edu
Url: www.princeton.edu/~ies

CONTENTS

FIGURES

G-3 EXCHANGE-RATE RELATIONSHIPS: A REVIEW OF THE RECORD AND OF PROPOSALS FOR CHANGE

1 Introduction

With the world only recently recovering from what has been compared to the worst international financial crisis of the last fifty years, there is renewed interest in rethinking and redesigning the global financial architecture. Trillions of dollars flow each day through the world's foreign-exchange and securities markets, making capital and the opportunity to diversify risk available around the world to borrowers and issuers deemed worthy of access. Although access to the international financial markets has expanded enormously in both scale and scope over the last decade (the international capital markets were simply off-limits to most private and many official borrowers and issuers in most countries until the early 1990s), the contagions following the December 1994 Mexican crisis and the June 1997 Thai crisis have made painfully clear how uncertain such access can be, even for countries with previously sound credit and growing, stable, well-managed economies.

Of course, it is not just in and among the emerging markets that turmoil has originated and contagion has spread. Japan has experienced two recessions during the decade and still has a fragile banking system and a mountain of government debt—much of it accumulated during a succession of unsuccessful fiscal-stimulus packages. Deflation continues in Japan, and short-term interest rates have fallen to just above absolute zero. The United States and Europe, although not themselves in the grip of financial and currency crises, have certainly not been immune to their effects. In the United States, the current-account deficit widened as exports to Asia and Latin America sagged and imports surged. In Europe, the deutsche mark and other European Monetary System (EMS) currencies strengthened as safe-haven capital flowed in, anticipating (correctly) the successful launch of the euro in January 1999, but not anticipating the slowdown in growth that would

This essay was prepared for the spring 1999 meeting of the Group of Thirty, which published a shorter version for a less specialized audience as Occasional Paper No. 59. I would like to thank Martin Feldstein, Linda Goldberg, Peter Kenen, Frederic Mishkin, Paul Volcker, David Walker, John Walsh, and seminar participants at the New York Federal Reserve and the Group of Thirty for sharing with me their views on this subject.

force the European Central Bank (ECB), in its first official action, to cut interest rates in the spring of 1999.

Many issues arise as part of any effort to rethink, let alone redesign, the global financial architecture. Recent papers on the subject have explored such topics as the regulation, supervision, and risk assessment of financial institutions engaged in international borrowing and lending (Calomiris, 1998); the role and function of the global capital market under the existing architecture (Obstfeld, 1998); the respective cases for capital controls (Bhagwati, 1998), currency unions (Dornbusch, 1999) and target zones (Williamson, 1998); the causes and consequences of currency crises (Krugman, 1997; Feldstein, 1999); and the role of the International Monetary Fund (IMF) with regard to all of these issues (Eichengreen, 1999).

This essay reviews exchange-rate relationships among the Group of Three (G-3) countries since the collapse of Bretton Woods and analyzes recent proposals for changing the way in which the G-3 conducts exchange-rate policy.[1] It seeks to understand these proposals within the context of the monetary policies and intervention arrangements that are likely to be pursued by the G-3 central banks in the absence of any formal arrangements among their governments to limit exchange-rate volatility.

Most countries outside the G-3 invoice a large portion of their international commerce, and denominate an even larger portion of their international borrowing, in a G-3 currency (especially dollars). The wide swings seen in bilateral G-3 exchange rates thus have large effects on the trade flows, capital flows, portfolio composition, and—as recent research demonstrates (Krugman, 1997)—the vulnerability to speculative attack in the many countries that choose to peg their exchange rates to the dollar, euro, or yen.[2] Notwithstanding the recent turmoil in international financial markets, the experience of economies such as Argentina and Hong Kong, which have weathered recent crisis contagions with currency boards, may make it more likely that other small open economies will adapt to the vicissitudes of the global capital market, not by adopting a flexible exchange rate, but by giving up monetary autonomy altogether and linking their money supplies and

[1] The original G-3 included Germany, Japan, and the United States. Since the euro was adopted as a common currency by eleven countries in January 1999, the G-3 has consisted of these countries, called collectively "Euroland," along with Japan and the United States.

[2] For this reason, McKinnon (1998) has recently characterized the yen-dollar exchange rate as the "loose cannon" behind the Asia crisis.

2

interest rates to a G-3 currency by way of a currency board or, even, complete "dollarization."[3]

The plan of this essay is as follows. Section 2 begins by reviewing the G-3 countries' experience with managed floating exchange rates since 1973. The future may not repeat the past, but with twenty-five years of data since the collapse of Bretton Woods, it is certainly possible to characterize the status quo and to make an educated guess about the likely future behavior of G-3 exchange rates under existing institutional arrangements. The section documents stylized facts of the post-Bretton Woods experience with managed floating, discusses the recent empirical research on the relation between exchange rates and fundamentals, examines some popular definitions of, and evidence for, currency misalignments, and reviews efforts following the Plaza Agreement to use intervention as a tool for dampening exchange-rate volatility.

Section 3 considers some of the criticisms of the post-Bretton Woods exchange-rate experience made by, among others, Krugman and Miller (1993), Volcker (1995), McKinnon (1997), and Williamson (1998). These and other papers argue that exchange-rate volatility appears to be excessive, that deviations of exchange rates from fundamental equilibrium values are persistent, that the costs of volatility and misalignment are not insignificant, and that benign neglect is an inappropriate policy response to (and may be one of the causes of) the observed wide fluctuations in G-3 exchange rates.

Section 4 describes the key features of five prominent proposals recently put forward by Volcker (1995), McKinnon (1997), Williamson (1998), and Wolf (1999). These proposals suggest that the G-3 countries adopt some form of target-zone system among themselves to keep exchange rates within a wide band surrounding their estimated equilibrium levels.

Section 5 outlines potential challenges to the durability of the proposed wide-band target-zone arrangements. These challenges include the possibility of conflicts between domestic and international objectives; the potential for conflicts among countries about the assignment of responsibility for adjusting monetary policy to maintain the target zone; the possibility of speculative attacks that exploit the difficulties countries face in making credible commitments to enforce target zones; the difficulties of conducting monetary policy when targeting an asset

---

[3] Dornbusch (1999), among others, has made this point. Obstfeld (1998) argues that, for many countries, there may not be a viable alternative between choosing a currency union with a G-3 country or allowing the exchange rate to float freely.

price such as an exchange rate; the uncertainties surrounding the estimate of the equilibrium exchange rate that must be used to define the central parity around which the bands are set; the particular challenges faced by Japan; and the degree of latitude that will be available for G-3 central banks to pursue independent monetary policies.

The essay concludes with Section 6 and two appendices. Appendix A reviews the way in which the best-known target-zone arrangement, the EMS, operated. The collapse of the original, narrow-band exchange-rate mechanism (ERM) of the EMS in 1992–93 made even many of the original EMS supporters, and certainly all of the original skeptics, doubtful about the sustainability of a target-zone system in a world of international capital mobility and divergent macroeconomic outcomes (caused perhaps, but not necessarily, by asymmetric shocks). The theoretical latitude to pursue independent monetary policy was not actually available to countries such as Britain when their business-cycle conditions called for interest rates below those in Germany (Clarida, Gali, and Gertler, 1998). After the summer of 1993, and until the parities of the European economic and monetary union (EMU) were frozen in late 1998, a wide band of plus or minus 15 percent of parity was adopted for the currencies that remained in the ERM. The ERM experience with wide bands is reviewed at the conclusion of the appendix.

Appendix B reviews the theoretical case for using a target-zone system as a way to reduce exchange-rate volatility. As is well known, a credible target zone for an exchange rate above its long-term equilibrium level can, in theory, deliver a "honeymoon" bonus that lessens the volatility of the exchange rate within the band. As Lars Svensson (1994a) has emphasized, moreover, a credible target zone can, in theory, provide some latitude for participating countries to pursue independent monetary policies while maintaining full international capital mobility.

2 G-3 Exchange Rates Since 1973

Figure 1 plots the history of monthly bilateral dollar, deutsche mark, and yen exchange rates since the collapse of Bretton Woods and the advent of (managed) floating in 1973. Figure 2 plots the recent, post-Louvre Accord history of these exchange rates, as well as the history of the (synthetic) euro, along with estimates of the purchasing-power-parity (PPP) levels of these exchange rates.[4] Over periods of several

---

[4] I use consumer-price indices (CPIs) to construct an estimate of the *changes* in the PPP exchange rate. To determine the *level* of the PPP exchange rate, I assume that the

years, the simple PPP relationship, $E = P/P^*$ (where P/P^* is the ratio of domestic to foreign price levels), appears, on average, to provide an anchor for these exchange rates (Frankel and Rose, 1996). However, not only have deviations from PPP been large, they have also been persistent and volatile. The short-term volatility of G-3 real exchange rates is one of most robust (and to many observers disturbing) characteristics of the post-Bretton Woods experience with floating exchange rates. It reflects, at least in part, the fact that nominal exchange rates are forward-looking asset prices that adjust continuously to clear the global capital market, whereas money-goods prices are often sticky and adjust only gradually to clear the international goods markets (Mussa, 1982; Dornbusch, [1976] 1992).

Purchasing-power parity is a useful construct for placing medium-term currency movements in context, but it is neither necessary nor sufficient for a currency to be properly aligned. Shifts in the supply of, or demand for, national outputs will usually require an adjustment in the terms of trade, or the relative price of nontraded goods, or both, and these relative-price adjustments will, in general, necessitate a departure from PPP (Obstfeld and Rogoff, 1997). Moreover, any required adjustment in the terms of trade or relative price of nontraded goods in response to a *real* disturbance will usually require an adjustment in the *nominal* exchange rate (Obstfeld, 1995). Clarida and Gali (1994) estimate a structural empirical model of the dollar-deutsche mark and dollar-yen exchange rates on data from the 1970s through the early 1990s. They decompose observed quarterly changes in bilateral real exchange rates into three sources: exchange-rate changes driven by shocks to money supply and demand ("asset-market" shocks), exchange-rate changes driven by shocks to the demand for national outputs ("demand" shocks), and exchange-rate changes driven by shocks to the supply of national outputs ("productivity" shocks). They conclude that a substantial portion of the short-term variance of real, as well as nominal, exchange-rate changes is caused by asset-market shocks.[5] They estimate, for example, that asset-market shocks account for 47 percent

---

bilateral exchange rates were at PPP in 1987, the year of the Louvre Accord. Results would be similar if I had used sample average deviations of an exchange rate from the ratio of CPIs.

[5] Clarida and Gali (1994) do not separately identify shocks to money supply and money demand, but they label a linear combination of these underlying disturbances as an asset-market shock. Eichenbaum and Evans (1995) use a different methodology to identify the importance of shocks to "monetary policy" and obtain similar results.

FIGURE 1
G-3 EXCHANGE RATES SINCE 1973

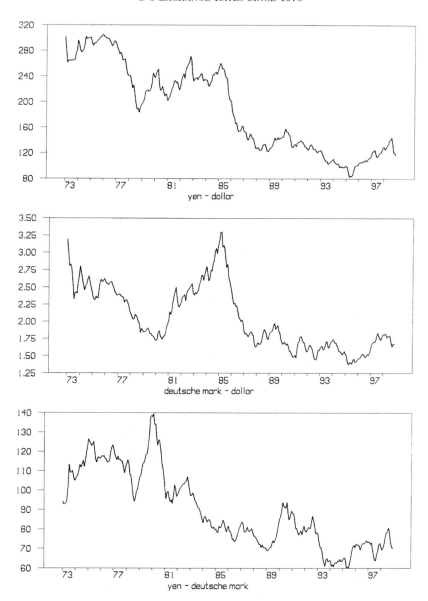

SOURCES: OECD, *Main Economic Indicators*, and author's calculations.

FIGURE 2

G-3 Exchange Rates Relative to Purchasing-Power Parity

SOURCES: OECD, *Main Economic Indicators*, and author's calculations.

of the variance of the three-month change in the dollar-deutsche mark real exchange rate and for 36 percent of the variance of the three-month change in the dollar-yen real exchange rate. Most of the remaining variance of real-exchange-rate changes is attributed to shocks in the relative demand for national outputs; very little (less than 10 percent) is attributed to productivity shocks. This does not mean that productivity shocks have been small; rather, it shows that it is only the country-specific component of productivity that drives the real exchange rate.

The Clarida-Gali model also provides a natural measure of when and to what extent the dollar-deutsche mark and dollar-yen exchange rates were overvalued or undervalued relative to their long-term equilibrium levels during the 1970s, 1980s, and early 1990s. In the Clarida-Gali model, the long-term equilibrium exchange rate is precisely defined: it is the multivariate Beveridge-Nelson (1981) permanent component of the real exchange rate adjusted by the multivariate Beveridge-Nelson permanent component of the ratio of U.S. to German or Japanese price levels. Intuitively, the Beveridge-Nelson permanent component of a time series is the long-horizon forecast of that series (adjusted for any drift) that is consistent with all restrictions that may be imposed on the multivariate macroeconomic model used to make the forecast.[6] The Clarida-Gali model does not impose any assumption or restriction on the long-term equilibrium exchange rate; for example, it does not assume that the equilibrium real exchange rate adjusts to achieve a particular level for the current-account balance in the long run.[7]

The Clarida-Gali (and, for that matter, any other) time-series method of estimating the long-term equilibrium real exchange rate cannot formally distinguish between two competing interpretations of the deviations of the exchange rate from the long-term equilibrium. According to the interpretation emphasized by Clarida and Gali (1994), these deviations do not represent exchange-rate misalignments but reflect, instead, the interplay of sticky-goods prices with nominal and real shocks that have transitory as well as permanent components. Another interpretation of such a decomposition is that the large and persistent departures from long-term equilibrium do represent misalignments.

Another, complementary, method of assessing the link between exchange rates and fundamentals in the G-3 has been taken by Nelson

[6] Cumby and Huizinga (1990) were the first to employ the multivariate Beveridge-Nelson decomposition approach to study exchange rates.

[7] This is the assumption used by Williamson (1994) and researchers at the IMF in constructing their estimates of "fundamental equilibrium exchange rates."

Mark (1995). Using the simple monetary model of exchange-rate determination as a starting point, Mark first confirms the widely held notion that quarter-to-quarter or even year-to-year changes in dollar-deutsche mark and dollar-yen nominal exchange rates during the post-Bretton Woods years have essentially been orthogonal to contemporaneous values of key fundamentals such as relative national money supplies and relative national outputs. At longer horizons of two, three, to four years, however, Mark finds striking evidence that cumulative nominal-exchange-rate changes are well explained by the initial deviation of the exchange rate from its "fundamental value." He estimates that if, in a given quarter, the dollar-deutsche mark or dollar-yen exchange rate is overvalued relative to the monetary-approach fundamentals, it will tend to depreciate, on average, until the initial overvaluation is eliminated in three or four years. Mark's point estimates suggest that between one-half and three-quarters of the variance of three- and four-year changes in nominal bilateral G-3 exchange rates are accounted for by this simple measure of initial over- or undervaluation relative to the flexible-price monetary-approach fundamentals. In Mark's words (1995, p. 210), "the improved fit attained as [the horizon] increases suggests that the noise that dominates quarter to quarter changes in [G-3 nominal exchange rates] averages out over long horizons."

The "noise" that dominates short-term changes in G-3 nominal exchange rates (both real and nominal) has not diminished appreciably over the last twenty-five years. Figure 3 depicts, for each bilateral nominal exchange rate, a rolling standard deviation of monthly logarithmic changes since 1977. The volatility of monthly changes in the yen-dollar and yen-deutsche mark exchange rates has risen during the 1990s to levels last observed during the early 1980s, and it is much higher than during the late 1970s. In recent years, however, there has been a substantial decline in the volatility of the deutsche mark-dollar exchange rate back to the ranges observed in the late 1970s. Figure 3 also shows that the recent volatility of the (synthetic) euro-dollar exchange rates leading up to EMU behaved similarly to deutsche mark-dollar volatilities.[8] The volatility actually occurring in G-3 exchange rates was greatly underestimated by early advocates of floating exchange rates such as Harry Johnson (Obstfeld, 1995).

The mere presence of this volatility (or its failure to diminish over time) is not, in itself, inconsistent with the notion that G-3 exchange

---

[8] The synthetic euro exchange-rate series is taken from the *Financial Times* and is constructed as a GDP-weighted average of the eleven bilateral EMU exchange rates with the dollar and yen.

FIGURE 3

EXCHANGE-RATE VOLATILITY

(*Rolling standard deviation of monthly changes*)

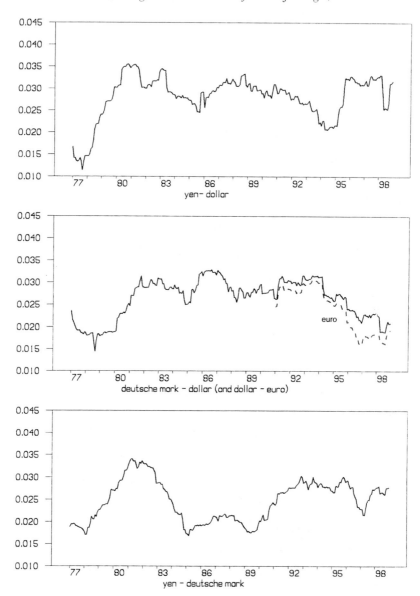

SOURCES: OECD, *Main Economic Indicators*, and author's calculations.

rates are determined in a rational, efficient asset market that responds only to actual "news" about fundamentals.[9] The Dornbusch ([1976] 1992) overshooting model links exchange-rate volatility to the jump in nominal exchange rates that occurs under rational expectations in response to a rise in the money supply or a fall in money demand that requires a divergence between the home and world interest rate. Another possible explanation for exchange-rate volatility is the fact that news about current fundamentals may also be providing information about the future growth rate of fundamentals, in which case the jumps in the exchange rate may (rationally) be more volatile than the news about current fundamentals (Mussa, 1982). Some of the recent empirical evidence presented in Clarida and Gali (1994) and Eichenbaum and Evans (1995) suggests that the level of overshooting or the magnification in response to an asset-market disturbance may be substantial. Clarida and Gali (1994) find that the immediate jump in the nominal exchange rate between the dollar and deutsche mark will be three times larger (4.5 percent) than the long-term depreciation in the exchange rate (1.5 percent) caused by a rise in money supply or a fall in money demand.

Although G-3 exchange rates since 1973 have exhibited wide swings and volatility that have failed to diminish over time, their determination has not been left entirely to the foreign-exchange markets. Periodically in the 1970s (most notably with the November 1978 dollar rescue package), and more frequently and systematically since 1985, the G-3 countries have led coordinated intervention operations to calm disorderly markets, to "lean against the wind," as their exchange rates drift away from the official perception of their fundamental equilibrium levels, or to "lean with the wind" to push exchange rates back to their fundamental equilibrium levels. Perhaps the most explicit, coordinated such effort was that of the February 1987 Louvre Accord, which established formal, but secret, target zones for the major currencies around their February 1987 levels. For at least several years after Louvre, new, but still secret, target zones were reestablished around new central parities that more accurately reflected the market realities of the time. Figures 4 and 5 present one prominent market maker's assessment of U.S. post-Louvre intervention strategy in the dollar-deutsche mark and dollar-yen markets.[10]

---

[9] This paragraph and the next two draw heavily on the discussions in Obstfeld (1995) and Dominguez and Frankel (1993).

[10] For the definitive account of G-3 intervention operations, see Dominguez and Frankel (1993).

FIGURE 4

U.S. INTERVENTION HISTORY: THE DOLLAR-MARK EXCHANGE RATE

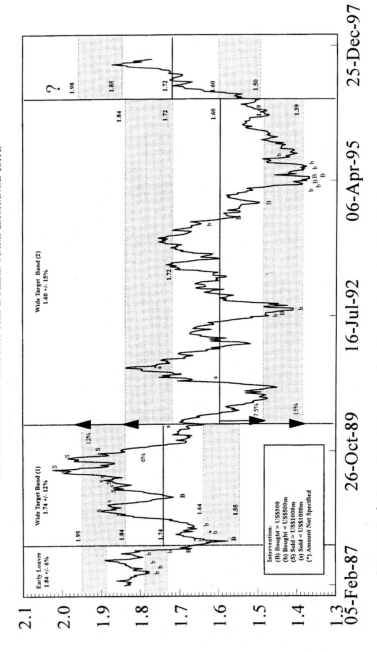

SOURCE: Credit Suisse First Boston; reproduced by permission from Prendergast, 1997, p. 16.

FIGURE 5

U.S. INTERVENTION HISTORY: THE DOLLAR-YEN EXCHANGE RATE

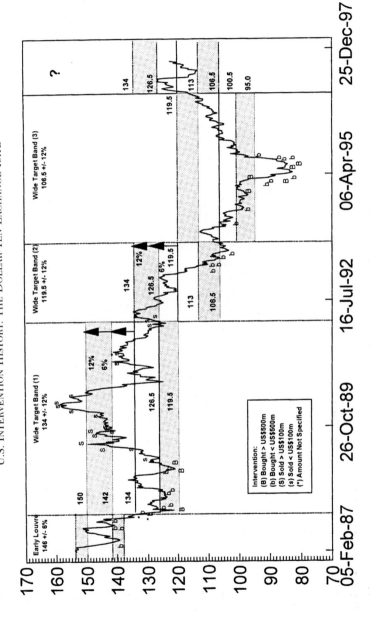

SOURCE: Credit Suisse First Boston; reproduced by permission from Prendergast, 1997, p. 17.

The conventional wisdom on sterilized foreign-exchange intervention is that its effects are expected to be small and short-lived unless supported by changes in monetary policies (Henderson and Sampson, 1983; Edison, 1993). This is essentially the position of the U.S. Treasury. To the extent that other researchers find a more significant role for sterilized intervention (Catte, Galli, and Rebecchini, 1992; Dominguez and Frankel, 1993), its influence is often attributed to its signaling effect. As stated by Dominguez and Frankel (1993, p. 139), "intervention operations—which after all are small compared with the private market—probably [can]not sustain control of the foreign exchange market for long without the sense of direction provided by monetary policy and might be used to pursue inconsistent policy goals even if such control could be sustained."

Which aspects of the exchange-rate experience of the old G-3 (Germany, Japan, United States) are most likely to characterize the experience of the new G-3 (Euroland, Japan, United States) in the absence of (and perhaps even after agreement to) any new arrangements among their governments to limit exchange-rate flexibility further? Notwithstanding the growing body of empirical evidence that the medium-term direction of bilateral exchange-rate movements has appropriately reflected the macroeconomic fundamentals, it will most likely continue to be true that the bulk of short-term exchange-rate volatility, and perhaps even the magnitude of medium-term exchange-rate swings, will be difficult to explain, even after the fact, by observed realizations of the fundamentals (Obstfeld, 1995). It will also likely continue to be true that the levels of bilateral G-3 exchange rates will often and persistently wander away from empirical estimates of their long-term equilibrium values, whether these are determined by a PPP relationship or by a more elaborate calculation of fundamental equilibrium levels that takes into account shifts in the terms of trade and sustainable current-account flows. Furthermore, there is reason to believe that the recent observed divergence between declining and modest dollar-euro volatility, on the one hand, and rising and high dollar-yen and euro-yen volatilities, on the other, may well continue. The United States and Euroland have similar inflation rates, are likely to have similar monetary-policy strategies, and are unlikely to subject the foreign-exchange markets to any large structural fiscal-policy surprises. The situation in Japan, by contrast, presents the markets with much more uncertainty. Until Japan's banking problems, deflation, and fiscal problems are (expected to be) resolved, wide swings in the yen-dollar and yen-euro exchange rates are not an unlikely prospect.

3 Criticisms of G-3 Exchange-Rate Experience Since 1973

Many if not most of the criticisms of the post-Bretton Woods experience with floating exchange rates—the "non" system, as it is sometimes called—begin with the presumption that much of the short-term volatility in exchange rates, and the failure of the volatility to diminish over time, is the result of "bandwagons," destabilizing speculation, herd behavior, and other pathologies of an international capital market that is thought to be far from efficient. John Williamson (1998, p. 2), for example, states that "the case for rejecting floating is based on the evidence that asset markets in general, and the foreign exchange markets in particular, are driven by herd behavior rather than rational expectation." Similarly, Paul Krugman and Marcus Miller (1993, pp. 313–314) argue that "there is no evidence supporting the view that exchange markets are efficient, or even that speculation will generally be stabilizing. We certainly have no grounds for dismissing the views of experienced market practitioners who warn of the potential for large exchange-rate swings that are unjustified by the fundamentals."

A second criticism of the post-Bretton Woods status quo follows from the presumption that an inefficient foreign-exchange market not only generates excessive short-term volatility but also produces significant and sustained misalignments of exchange rates relative to the levels supported by the fundamentals when these excessive short-term exchange-rate changes cumulate over time.

Many authors think that the costs of excessive exchange-rate volatility are made manageable, although not trivial, by the ready and ever-increasing availability of financial derivative products for hedging short- and medium-term foreign-exchange exposure.[11] But hedging entails costs, especially as the horizon lengthens, and it is not always possible when the foreign-currency cash inflows or outflows to be hedged are themselves uncertain. The costs of exchange-rate misalignments, if they are as common and sizable as some suggest, are believed to be "extremely harmful to macroeconomic stability and microeconomic efficiency" (McKinnon and Ohno, 1997, p. 52). By altering international relative prices (the terms of trade), domestic relative prices (of non-traded goods), and the prices of traded commodities relative to traded differentiated products through a process Ronald McKinnon and Kenichi Ohno (1997) label "price diffusion," excessive exchange-rate volatility and persistent misalignments are often held responsible for depressing

---

[11] See Kenen and Rodrik, [1986] 1994; Goldberg and Kolstad, 1995; and Campa and Goldberg, 1999, for empirical estimates of the costs of exchange-rate volatility.

bilateral trade flows, distorting investment decisions, and misallocating the outsourcing locations chosen by multinational firms. Moreover, because most countries outside the G-3 peg their exchange rates to the euro, yen, or (overwhelmingly) the dollar, the considerable volatility in the bilateral G-3 exchange rates has significant effects on the trade flows, capital flows, portfolio composition, and vulnerability to speculative attack in these countries. Paul Volcker (1995, p. 8) sums up well (and presciently) the essence of these criticisms of the existing nonsystem:

> There is a reluctance to make a sufficiently strong commitment to [exchangerate] stability for fear the effort could fail, at political and economic cost. What is not adequately weighed in the balance is the disintegrating force of present exchange rate arrangements, with its inherent uncertainties and false pricing signals. The irony . . . is to observe the enormous energy and political capital dedicated in recent years to reducing already low tariffs to minimal levels, only to see the potential gains in efficiency and trade overwhelmed by the volatility of exchange markets. In the same vein, in all our discussions of the problems of development . . . of emerging economies, we don't give much weight to their stake in more stable exchange markets.

4 Recent Proposals for Limiting G-3 Exchange-Rate Volatility

In 1993, following the collapse of the ERM, the IMF published a study (Goldstein et al., 1993) that outlined several suggestions, gleaned from talks with government officials and market participants, for improving the operation and durability of international agreements to limit exchange-rate volatility and prevent misalignments. Because several of these ideas are embodied in the recent proposals to limit exchange-rate volatility among the G-3, and because the G-3 proposals are meant to make any future arrangements more durable than the ERM turned out to be (see Appendix A), I begin the analysis of the new proposals by discussing some of the policies that were suggested in the aftermath of the ERM crisis.[12]

The first suggestion made in the IMF report was for target-zone arrangements to have more frequent (and smaller) changes of central parities within the band. The aim was to design a coordination process that would produce timely agreement on the need for small, systematic, adjustments in central parities, one that would depoliticize these adjustments and restore the "two-way bet" for speculators. One goal of this strategy was to reduce greatly the need for large realignments and

---

[12] This paragraph and the next three draw heavily on Goldstein et al. (1993, pp. 17–20).

to put more responsibility for exchange-rate changes "in the hands of technicians" (Goldstein et al., 1993, p. 19). Another goal was to allow the exchange rate to do more of the work in allowing a country to adjust to real shocks; this, it was hoped, would reduce the need for countries to agree on interest-rate changes.

The second suggestion contained in the IMF report was for target zones to feature wider bands. The goal was to discourage "one-way bets," to allow the exchange rate a greater role in facilitating macroeconomic adjustment, and to provide some leeway for central banks to pursue interest-rate policies tailored to domestic macroeconomic circumstances.

The third suggestion offered in the report was to urge policymakers to build up the credibility of the target-zone arrangement by taking action to convey their preferences for exchange-rate stability; policymakers were encouraged "to build up credibility gradually by showing the markets that *whenever there is a potential conflict between the internal and external requirements for monetary policy, the exchange rate is king.* Once the markets learn that countries are not schizophrenic about monetary policy and that exchange rate adjustments— when they occur—will be small, attacks will cease" (Goldstein, 1993, p. 20; emphasis added).

The report also discussed the doubts that can be raised about this option and, in particular, noted that building credibility in this way would put a great deal of weight on the coordination of interest-rate changes in a world in which significant differences exist between the internal and external requirements for monetary policy. Another important issue was whether or not it would even be possible to build credibility for a wide-band arrangement if the markets (rationally?) expected that central banks in countries such as the United States and in Euroland would put inflation and output-stability goals ahead of the exchange-rate objective when these goals come into conflict.

Outlined below are the essential ingredients of five proposals offered by Volcker (1995), McKinnon (1997), Williamson (1998), and Wolf (1999) to limit the volatility of, and prevent misalignments in, G-3 exchange rates. For completeness, I begin with the status quo following the Plaza Agreement.

The Post-Plaza Status Quo

McKinnon ((1997, p. 531) notes that the post–Plaza status quo arrangements among the G-3 were, for several years following the Louvre Accord in February 1987, characterized by a general inclination to set broad target zones for the deutsche mark-dollar and yen-dollar exchange rates in the range of plus or minus 10 to 12 percent of central parity. The central parities were not announced and the zonal boundaries remained "flexible." As disparities in economic fundamentals emerged, the central parities were adjusted (although it is not known how often, because the adjustments were confidential). Even after the zones were abandoned (and reliable sources claim they were never really in force), there have continued to be occasional coordinated intervention operations for the purpose of reversing short-term trends (leaning against the wind) when a bilateral exchange rate has become sufficiently misaligned so as to cause concern among officials. These coordinated interventions have generally been conducted publicly, rather than in secret. As a rule, the domestic monetary impact of these interventions has been sterilized immediately so as to leave short-term interest rates unchanged. Domestic monetary policies in each country have been devoted to achieving and maintaining a low, but positive, stable rate of inflation.[13]

None of the G-3 countries is an explicit targeter of public inflation, but all three G-3 central banks have in the past appeared to pursue what Clarida, Gali, and Gertler (1998) dub "soft-hearted" inflation-forecast targeting: a strategy that sets short-term interest rates with the aim of stabilizing both expected inflation and deviations of output from potential. It is important to note that no G-3 central bank, including the pre-EMU Bundesbank, has pursued a price-level targeting objective. When inflation has overshot or undershot its implicit target, the price level has been rebased for the purpose of targeting the next year's inflation (Clarida and Gertler, 1997). The G-3 countries have not, to this point, appeared to coordinate their implicit inflation targets, although both the U.S. Federal Reserve and the European Central Bank (ECB) are thought to have a target of 2 percent for CPI inflation.

There is more uncertainty about the aims of the newly independent Bank of Japan. As the June 1997 *Report of the G-7 Finance Ministers* (quoted in Cross, 1998, p. 117) states:

---

[13] This is not to say that these policies have always been successful. Japan, in particular, is hindered by a fragile banking system and a significant debt burden. Notwithstanding a parade of cuts in the short-term interest rate by the Bank of Japan to its current level of 0.0002 per annum, Japanese monetary policy during the 1990s has failed to produce low and stable inflation and has contributed, instead, to persistent deflation in producer prices over the last several years. McKinnon and Ohno (1997) and Cargill, Hutchison, and Ito (1997) provide superb and detailed accounts of the challenges faced by the Bank of Japan during the 1990s. See also Krugman (1997).

Exchange rate misalignments can heighten uncertainty in the global economy and can be detrimental to growth and trade. When exchange rates appear to move out of line with underlying fundamentals, close monitoring is necessary and coordinated responses may be required. We should continue our close cooperation in exchange markets with this foundation, taking into account the fact that

- A clear and consistent articulation of a common G7 view can have a stabilizing influence [on exchange rates];
- interventions can be effective in certain circumstances, especially when they reinforce changes in policies and/or underlying fundamentals that lead to changes in market expectations about future exchange rates;
- the instrument of intervention must be used judiciously, given its implications for monetary policy and the amount that the authorities can mobilize relative to the size of the international capital markets. Nevertheless, these factors do not impede our joint ability to send a clear message to the markets, if and when appropriate;
- interventions are more likely to be effective when they are concerted and reflect a common assessment.

The Volcker (1995) Proposal

In his Stamp lecture presented at London University in 1995, Paul Volcker (1995, p. 7) called for a set of G-3 exchange-rate arrangements that would "moderate and reverse exchange rate fluctuations among the key currencies before they become extreme, rather than being forced to respond defensively, after substantial risk to the world economy is already evident." Volcker's proposal contains the following provisions.

First, the participating countries (Euroland, Japan, and the United States), in consultation with the IMF, would reach a consensus on "broadly appropriate equilibrium values" for their nominal bilateral exchange rates. These would be the central parities of the new system. Actual nominal bilateral exchange rates would be allowed to fluctuate within a target zone of plus or minus 10 percent around these central parities. There would be an initial transition period during which fluctuations of up to plus or minus 15 percent would be permitted.

Second, the G-3 countries would need to be prepared *jointly* to defend the target zones with intervention, on a substantial scale if necessary. Inframarginal intervention would not be discouraged.

Third, the proposal recognizes that sterilized intervention would almost certainly not always be enough, even with wide bands, to maintain the integrity of the target zone. Thus, the Volcker proposal (1995, p. 7) calls for the G-3 central banks to "modify their monetary policies in support of the exchange rate objective" and states (p. 8):

Relatively wide and potentially movable exchange rate ranges are in a sense a compromise between the logical extremes of fixed and floating rates. The idea, for all its analytical appeal, does not lend itself to slogans or sound bites, nor to instinctive political or public support. The question will be asked, when the defense of the range is required, if 10 percent is all right, what about 11 or 12 or more? Is it really worth spending money in the exchange markets, modifying monetary policy, and taking care to balance the budget just to save another percentage point or two?

The answer must be yes. What is at issue is not that last percent but whether governments will succeed in inducing the market itself to stabilize exchange rates. The success or failure in that effort is plainly dependent on the credibility of official intentions. But when that credibility is established, markets will work with governments, not against them, to maintain a sense of equilibrium.

Although the proposal states clearly that countries will, at least on occasion, need to modify their monetary policies in support of the exchange-rate commitment, it does not indicate whether this responsibility should be assigned to the weak-currency or to the strong-currency country. The proposal does, however, call for the IMF to work with and, when necessary, lead the G-3 countries in determining a course of action for coordinating the changes in monetary or fiscal policies that are necessary to support the exchange-rate objective.[14]

The Volcker proposal (1995, p. 7) recognizes that "the extent to which countries are prepared to announce publicly the 'equilibrium ranges' and the frequency with which they might be modified are sensitive points," yet it seems clear that Volcker intends that the target zone for nominal bilateral G-3 exchange rates be publicly announced (perhaps after a transition period?). Volcker argues, moreover, that an appeal of the wide-band target zone is that it facilitates making any changes necessary in the central parities in a manner that minimizes the possibilities of one-way bets. It calls for such changes to be made, whenever possible, in amounts that are substantially smaller than the width of the band, so that the exchange rate need not move much, or perhaps at all, when such adjustments are made.

The Williamson Proposals

Williamson, more than anyone else, has promoted the implementation of a target-zone arrangement using wide bands around exchange-rate

---

[14] In this regard, the IMF would play the role of resolving "commitment and coordination problems" (see Eichengreen and Kenen, 1994).

levels that are consistent with medium-term equilibrium in the current account. In a recent article, Williamson (1998) outlined two proposals for creating such a system: one suggesting a moving- or "crawling"-band system and another suggesting a system of "monitoring" bands.

According to Williamson (1998), a moving band requires that a central bank undertake a public obligation to maintain the exchange rate within a wide, publicly announced band (of plus or minus 10 percent or even 15 percent) around a parity that is periodically adjusted in small steps so as to keep the band in line with fundamentals. Williamson envisions three factors that would contribute to a systematic adjustment, or crawl, in the central parity. First, a country would want to adjust the nominal exchange rate by the amount of the inflation differential with the other country or, in the case of a central parity expressed in terms of a basket, the other countries with which the home country is trying to stabilize the exchange rate. Second, a country might want its central parities to adjust gradually so as to allow for a real appreciation following a rise in aggregate demand or for a real depreciation following a fall in aggregate demand. Third, a country with a rapid rise of productivity in the traded-goods sector relative to the service sector might wish to offset the Balassa-Samuelson effect with a gradual nominal appreciation of the exchange rate.[15]

To pin down the central parity, Williamson suggests deriving it from an estimate of the real, effective exchange rate that would be consistent with macroeconomic balance in the medium term. Macroeconomic balance, in turn, requires both internal balance (full employment) and external balance. External balance is defined as a current-account deficit (or surplus) that is sustainable and consistent with the medium-term current-account positions of other countries (Williamson and Henning, 1994). Although, in practice, many countries choose a central parity expressed as a bilateral nominal exchange rate, and much of the discus-

---

[15] The Balassa-Samuelson effect states that workers in tradables in poor countries are less productive than their counterparts in rich countries but that productivity in nontradables is comparable across countries. For many years, Japan has experienced a trend real appreciation of the yen that has been attributed to the Balassa-Samuelson effect. This might suggest allowing for a gradual appreciation of the nominal yen exchange rate as part of a Williamson moving-band system. Much recent discussion, however, including the in-depth studies by McKinnon and Ohno (1997) and Cargill, Hutchison, and Ito (1997) are quite critical of the syndrome of the "ever-higher yen" and the deflationary force that they attribute to it. For this reason, McKinnon (1998) calls for a constant yen-dollar central parity, and Wolf (1999) calls for a floor on the yen-dollar rate, which would, in the face of the Balassa-Samuelson effect, require Japan to have faster-trend CPI inflation than the United States has.

sion about future G-3 exchange-rate arrangements presumes that such arrangements would be defined in terms of bilateral nominal G-3 exchange rates, Williamson (1998, p. 8) points out that choosing a bilateral nominal exchange rate "has the advantage of simplicity, but it can also have a severe disadvantage for a country with a diversified trading pattern." For this reason, some countries, such as Chile, establish central parities with respect to baskets of currencies of their major trading partners. Indeed, Williamson (1986, p. 166) was explicit in his earlier writings in recommending that the leading countries "negotiate a set of mutually consistent target [zones] for their [nominal] effective exchange rates." It makes sense to focus on effective exchange rates (Williamson, 1986), because it is real effective exchange rates that, with a lag, influence trade flows and aggregate demand.[16] As will be discussed below, the nominal trade-weighted dollar has, over the last eleven years, rarely—and then only briefly—departed from a band of plus or minus 10 percent of its 1988 level. This is also essentially true for the trade-weighted deutsche mark. The trade-weighted yen, by contrast, has often persistently and substantially fluctuated by much more than plus or minus 10 percent of its 1988 level and, for reasons that are well known, has closely mimicked the yen-dollar exchange rate.

Announcing the band implies a commitment to intervene at the margins to prevent the rate from going outside the band. However, Williamson states that most countries that operate wide bands—and, we would add, the EMS countries that were operating with much narrower bands (Svensson, 1992)—also make a practice of intervening within the margins, typically to discourage the rate from approaching the edge of the band. This practice is in contrast to the original theoretical target-zone models, which assumed away inframarginal interventions and thus implied that the exchange rate would spend most of its time near the edge of the band (Bertola and Caballero, 1992). Indeed, as Svensson (1994a) points out, target-zone systems that have succeeded in stabilizing exchange rates have done so by committing monetary policy (which sometimes appears as nonsterilized intervention) to that objective, so as to keep the exchange rate within the band, even when it is already inside it. Williamson (1998, p. 10) acknowledges that "intervention alone is unlikely to suffice to defend a band against strong market pressure. The next line of defense is usually to change monetary policy, tightening

[16] However, any distortions in investment decisions or multinational outsourcing decisions that arise from "misaligned" exchange rates are likely to be related to persistent, bilateral misalignments. The distortions would not "cancel out," even if the bilateral misalignments did so on a trade-weighted, multilateral basis.

it when the problem is a too weak currency." Williamson (1998) is silent about the assignment of responsibility in cases in which more than one currency threatens to breach its target zone.[17] In earlier work, however, Williamson (1986, p. 167) endorsed "a regime of discretion, whereby the strong currency countries would act [to depreciate their currencies] if the participating countries judged that deflation posed a more serious global threat than inflation, and the weak currency countries would act [to appreciate their currencies] in the converse case."

Williamson (1998) provides three reasons to support a wide-band arrangement. The first is that the band needs to be wide because estimates of equilibrium exchange rates are imprecise. The second (discussed in Appendix B) is that a wide band can, in theory, give scope for cyclical variations in monetary policy to influence short-term interest rates. However, even a fully credible wide band of plus or minus 10 percent allows for only modest differences in long-term, say ten-year, yields. In fact, if the expectations hypothesis of the term structure is correct, and the long rate is an arithmetic average of current and expected future short-term interest rates, it follows that if the band width from central parity is $\chi = 0.10$ and it takes n years for rates to return to global levels, the maximum differential in the yields to maturity on a domestic and foreign ten-year bond will always be 100 basis points.[18] The third reason Williamson cites for a wide band is "to contain speculative pressures." According to Williamson (1998, p. 9), "the wider the band, the greater the possibility of a rebound in the rate and hence the possible cost of an unsuccessful attack, and the less is the possibility that speculators will catch the authorities in the no-win situation of having to try and defend a disequilibrium rate."

[17] Note that if the central parities are defined in terms of nominal effective exchange rates, as called for by Williamson (1986), it can easily be (and often has been) the case that the nominal effective dollar remains comfortably within a plus or minus 10 percent band while the nominal effective yen wanders far away from any such band.

[18] In general, if central parity is to be restored in n years, uncovered interest parity implies that the maximum cumulative interest differential is

$$(R^*_{t,1} - R_{t,1}) + (R^*_{t+1,1} - R_{t+1,1}) + \ldots + (R^*_{t+n-1,1} - R_{t+n-1,1}) = \chi .$$

The expectations hypothesis of the term structure, for a maturity of L years, yields

$$R_{t,L} = (1/L)(R_{t,1} + \ldots + R_{t+n-1,1} + R^*_{t+n,1} + \ldots + R^*_{t+L-1,1})$$

$$R^*_{t,L} = (1/L)(R^*_{t,1} + \ldots + R^*_{t+n-1,1} + R^*_{t+n,1} + \ldots + R^*_{t+L-1,1}) .$$

Subtracting, for any $n \leq L$, and for any sequence of interest differentials that satisfies the expectation that central parity will be restored in n years, we obtain

$$R^*_{t,L} - R_{t,L} = \chi/L .$$

Thus, if n = three years, zonal boundaries of 0.1 permit one-year interest rates to fall 333 basis points below those in the rest of the system for each of three years.

Williamson (1998, p. 7) also outlines a closely related proposal for a monitoring band. The key difference between the moving wide band just discussed and a monitoring band is that "the latter does not involve an obligation to defend the edge of the band. There is a presumption that the authorities will normally intervene to discourage the rate from straying far from the band, but they have a whole extra degree of flexibility in deciding the tactics that they will employ to achieve this. In particular, if they decide that market pressures are overwhelming, they can choose to allow the rate to take the strain even if this involves the rate going outside the band." Williamson suggests that the width of a monitoring band should be narrower, say, plus or minus 5 percent, than the width chosen for a target zone with "hard" margins (plus or minus 10 percent), because under the former, there is no obligation to defend the band, but only a promise to start defending the band once the margin has been crossed. According to Williamson (1998, p. 12), the "advantage of [a monitoring band] is that it would avoid drawing a sharp line in the sand, whose breach gives a signal to the market that policy has failed and all bets are now off." Again, Williamson is silent on the assignment of responsibility in the cases in which more than one currency threatens to breach its monitoring zone.

The McKinnon Proposal

McKinnon's (1997) recently proposed "common monetary standard for the 21st century [CMS21]" is among the most ambitious and fully articulated proposals for a new G-3 exchange-rate and monetary regime. This is so, notwithstanding the fact that it was published in 1997, before EMU came into existence. If anything, however, EMU makes it easier to interpret McKinnon's proposal. If "ECB" is substituted for "Bundesbank," and "Euroland" for "Germany," McKinnon's proposal includes the following elements. First, the G-3 would publicly announce a target zone for the bilateral dollar-yen and dollar-euro exchange rates of plus or minus 5 percent around central parities that are consistent with PPP for traded manufactures. Second, the G-3 would defend these parities through nonsterilized (or only partly sterilized) intervention. The arrangement would be entirely symmetric. If the yen were to weaken against the dollar, for example, the Bank of Japan would be expected to tighten Japanese monetary policy by selling dollars and buying yen, thus draining reserves from the Japanese banking system by raising short-term yen interest rates. Similarly, the Federal Reserve would be expected to ease U.S. monetary policy by selling dollars and buying yen, thus adding reserves to the U.S. banking system and lowering short-term

24

dollar interest rates. McKinnon recommends, in light of the evidence presented by Dominguez and Frankel (1993), that these joint nonsterilized interventions be publicly announced so as to enhance their signaling value. Third, the G-3 central banks would, under the McKinnon proposal, jointly commit to a price-level target for their respective producer-price indices (PPIs). When combined with the commitment to a central parity determined by the initial PPP exchange rates between the United States and Euroland, this would require not only that the Federal Reserve, the ECB, and the Bank of Japan have a common inflation target, but also that they not rebase their price-level targets following an overshooting or undershooting of PPI inflation. Thus, for simplicity, if the agreed upon common PPI inflation target is zero, then in a year in which U.S. PPI inflation was 2 percent, the Federal Reserve would, in the following year, be mandated to tighten monetary policy so as to achieve a 2 percent deflation in the U.S. PPI. McKinnon does not expect that this price-level target would conflict with the nominal-exchange-rate target, because he believes that PPP for traded goods *is* the equilibrium exchange rate as long as the markets believe that central banks will target PPP.

McKinnon explicitly recognizes that his proposal—and we would add, any target-zone proposal—is vulnerable to speculative attack. In particular, he states (1997, p. 518) that, "the waves of speculation that swept the EMS in September 1992 and again in August 1993 are indications of what might happen to CMS21 in a broader context. . . . When international capital markets are wide open, such speculative attacks—warranted or unwarranted—on particular currencies can't be ruled out." McKinnon's proposal explicitly allows for an escape clause: a country is allowed to suspend "temporarily" its promise to devote monetary policy to keeping its bilateral exchange rates within a band defined by PPP. However, McKinnon's "restoration rule" calls for the wayward country to devote monetary policy to restoring the PPI price level prevailing when the suspension occurred before it may reenter the exchange-rate arrangement at the original parity.

The Wolf Proposal

In an article last year in the *Financial Times*, Martin Wolf (1999) outlined a proposal—which draws in part from ideas presented by McKinnon (1998) and Krugman (1998a)—for Japan and Euroland to set a unilaterally enforced ceiling on their respective bilateral nominal exchange rates with the dollar. That is, the Bank of Japan would agree to conduct monetary policy in such a way as to prevent the yen-dollar exchange rate from strengthening beyond some specified level, say, 110 yen to the dollar (the level suggested by Wolf), but would not be required (as in a target zone) to prevent the yen from weakening beyond some upper threshold for the yen-dollar exchange rate. Similarly, the ECB would agree to conduct monetary policy in such a way as to prevent the dollar-euro exchange rate from strengthening beyond, say, 1.3 dollars to the euro (a level at which the euro would be roughly 10 percent stronger than it was when launched). Again, there would no additional commitment for the ECB to prevent the euro from weakening beyond some lower threshold for the dollar-euro exchange rate. There would thus be no central parities to defend, and a currency depreciation in Japan or Euroland that coincided with a slumping economy would not mandate a tightening of monetary policy to defend a band that did not exist.

Unlike other proposals in which the goal is to achieve exchange-rate stability and prevent currency misalignments while trying to provide some leeway for countries to pursue their own monetary policies, the idea behind the Wolf proposal is to constrain monetary policy in certain countries in the world where it is feared that, because the central banks wish to demonstrate their independence, monetary policy is contributing to deflation and stagnation. Note the asymmetry. According to Wolf (1999, p. 11):

> Neither the ECB [n]or the Bank of Japan is at all likely to start an inflationary spree. Thus, there seems little need for exchange rate floors. Ceilings on the appreciation of the yen and euro against the dollar are a different matter. . . . The Japanese case is clear. Convincing the Japanese public that there is a ceiling to the yen's rate against the dollar would be the single most effective way of eliminating the specter of deflation. . . . [With an exchange rate ceiling,] Japanese inflation could not then be consistently below that in the US. This would make it easier for Japanese authorities to establish negative real rates of interest, if and when needed. What about Europe? . . . The ECB's price stability objective may similarly prove compatible with stagnation. . . . Against such a background, a threat by the European finance ministers to impose a ceiling on the euro's rate against the dollar seems at least a sensible tactic. . . . The ECB will protest furiously. But the ministers can, it appears, override such objections—or agree to drop the proposal in return for an inflation target of, say, 2 percent.

5   Challenges Facing Efforts to Limit Exchange-Rate Volatility

So what is the dilemma of the international financial architecture? It is that, essentially because of the threat of currency speculation, you can't get everything you want. More specifically, insisting on having any one of the three desirable attributes in an international regime . . . adjustment, confidence, and liquidity . . . forces the abandonment of one of the others. As a result, there is a limited menu of possible regimes—and each item on that menu is unsatisfactory in some important way (Krugman, 1998b, p. 1).

An essential appeal of the proposals reviewed above derives from their promise to relax the constraint imposed by the "impossible trinity" of international finance: the impossibility that international capital mobility (liquidity), stable exchange rates (confidence), and independent national monetary policies (adjustment) can coexist. How can these proposals promise to resolve the dilemma cited by Krugman? They can do so by permitting central banks to adjust short-term interest rates in line with domestic macroeconomic conditions without resorting to capital controls, and to do this while maintaining exchange-rate stability (at least within the width of the bands) and perhaps also by benefiting from the honeymoon bonus predicted by the target-zone models. A credible target zone reduces the opportunities for one-way bets against a central bank while still promising to rule out extreme exchange-rate fluctuations (see Appendix B). If speculators expect intervention and the commitment of monetary policy to the exclusive goal of defending the zonal boundaries, the target zone will deliver an added benefit by stabilizing intraband movements without the need to devote monetary policy to that goal when the exchange rate is within the band. A credible wide band thus gives policymakers more scope for active monetary policy when it is most needed, and this, in turn, enhances the credibility of the arrangement that was necessary for (limited) monetary autonomy in the first place. Thus, it is sometimes argued, a "virtuous circle" may result, or, in the words of Obstfeld and Rogoff (1995, p. 91), "target zones would thus appear to provide a good practical balance between the seeming chaos of flexible rates and the straightjacket of fixed rates."[19]

Notwithstanding the potential of the proposals reviewed in Section 4, skeptics (including Obstfeld and Rogoff) argue that arrangements for limiting exchange-rate volatility are not likely to fulfill their promise without confronting the constraints of the impossible trinity. In particular, it is argued that, as long as countries put priority on maintaining unfettered access to the international capital market, and as long as the markets have some doubt that the "exchange rate [will be] king" whenever a conflict arises between the internal and external requirements for monetary policy, any agreement to limit exchange-rate

---

[19] This paragraph and the next draw heavily on the discussion in Obstfeld and Rogoff (1995).

volatility by adopting target zones, even those with wide bands, will not be durable and "may be little more than a placebo, differing in principle from a freely floating exchange rate only to the extent that it affects market psychology" (Obstfeld and Rogoff, 1995, p. 92).

A number of possible challenges to the durability of a wide-band target zone will be discussed below. They include:

- conflicts that may arise between domestic and international objectives;
- conflicts that may arise among countries about the assignment of responsibility for adjusting monetary policy to maintain the target zone;
- the possibility of speculative attacks that exploit the difficulty countries face in making credible commitments to enforce target zones, given competing domestic and international objectives;
- difficulties in conducting monetary policy when targeting an asset price such as an exchange rate;
- uncertainties surrounding the estimate of the equilibrium exchange rate that is used to define the central parity around which the bands are set;
- the particular challenges faced by Japan in credibly committing to exchange-rate stability in the context of ongoing deflation, a yawning output gap, huge budget deficits, and a newly independent central bank seeking to distance itself from the ministry of finance;
- the limited degree of latitude that may be available for G-3 central banks to pursue independent monetary policies if they wish to reduce exchange-rate volatility.

The Potential Conflict between Domestic and International Objectives

A virtue of the proposals discussed in the previous section is that they explicitly recognize the conflicts that can arise between domestic and international objectives. As Obstfeld and Rogoff (1995) emphasize, target-zone systems are not fragile because central banks *cannot* tighten monetary policy sufficiently to enforce them; they are fragile because central bankers (and the executives who appoint them and the legislators who pass the laws that define their mandates) are *unwilling* "to cling to an exchange rate target without regard to what is happening in the rest of the economy" (Obstfeld and Rogoff, 1995, p. 79).

Depending on the stage of the business cycle and the constellation of shocks that have hit the economy, the exchange-rate commitment may not always, or even most of the time, be in conflict with the other goals of monetary policy. This appears to have been true for the United States in 1995, when the (trade-weighted) dollar was very weak, for Germany in 1995–96, when the (trade-weighted) mark was very strong, and for the United States in 1998, when the (trade-weighted) dollar was very strong. However, history is full of instances in which domestic objectives and the exchange-rate target do come into conflict. For example, as shown in Appendix A, conflicts between domestic stabilization objectives and the commitment to the (narrow-band) EMS were the proximate cause of the 1992 crisis (Clarida, Gali, and Gertler, 1998).

Conflicts about the Responsibility for Adjusting Monetary Policy

All five of the proposals recognize that, under certain circumstances, the zonal boundaries will come under pressure caused by the weakness of one currency relative to at least one other currency. For the proposals that define central parities by bilateral nominal exchange rates (say, relative to the dollar), it is true that when one currency is weak and at one edge of the band, at least one other currency is strong and at the other edge of the band. For the arrangements that define central parities in terms of nominal effective exchange rates, this will not always be the case. When it is, however, it will be necessary for the countries involved to agree on an assignment of responsibility for changing national monetary policies so as to maintain the integrity of the band. The McKinnon (1997) proposal is explicit about the assignment that would be required, calling for symmetric adjustment in both the weak-currency country (which would need to tighten monetary policy) and the strong-currency country (which would need to ease policy). The Wolf (1999) proposal would require, for example, that Japan and Germany ease unilaterally if their currencies were to strengthen sufficiently against the dollar. The other proposals are less explicit about assigning the burden of adjustment. History indicates that, in practice, weak-currency countries have often sought to put pressure on strong-currency countries to ease monetary policy, but that their efforts have usually been rebuffed, generally because such a change in policy would conflict with domestic policy objectives in the strong-currency country. There is also a broader point to consider. Since the end of the gold standard, there has been no example of a fixed-exchange-rate or target-zone system that has been maintained by means of symmetric adjustments of national monetary policies and open capital accounts.

Speculative Attacks Driven by Market Doubts about the Commitment to Defend the Zone

During the ERM crisis, short-term interest rates in Sweden were raised to 500 percent (on an annualized basis), and short-term interest rates in

Italy were estimated to be 1,000 basis points higher than warranted by domestic macroeconomic conditions (Clarida, Gali, and Gertler, 1998, and Appendix A). In neither case was this enough, and both countries allowed their currencies to float. A promise to ignore the effects of such high interest rates on the banking system, and on investment and employment, may well not be credible. If the markets attach some positive probability (possibly less than one) that the target zone is not credible, even a wide-band target zone may become vulnerable to speculative attack. In particular, Obstfeld and Rogoff (1995, p. 91) argue that although "a wide band may postpone the day of reckoning on which the exchange rate comes under attack, it does not postpone it forever. When the zone's boundaries are reached, maintaining them in the face of speculative pressure presents all the problems of a fixed exchange rate."[20]

Why might G-3 promises to maintain exchange rates within wide-band target zones not be credible? Several reasons, additional to those mentioned above, might cause doubt. First, the markets recognize that, at some time in the future, domestic and exchange-rate objectives may come into conflict and that G-3 members may squabble about the assignment of responsibility to change monetary policy. In the absence of a history in which the exchange rate has been "king," the markets may well expect past behavior to continue should future conflicts arise. Indeed, the IMF *Capital Markets Report* (Goldstein et al., 1993) quoted above explicitly acknowledges that this is the likely outcome. Under such circumstances, and given the logic of the second-generation speculative-attack models reviewed in Appendix A, an attack may be expected to occur well before the fundamentals themselves would even tempt a country to abandon its exchange-rate commitment.

There is a real possibility of a "vicious circle" occurring. Suppose a wide band is announced but that, for the reasons discussed above, it is not initially credible. Now let fundamentals, not speculators, push the exchange rate to weaken the edge of the band. Because the band is not credible, and perhaps also because policymakers will argue about who must tighten and who must ease monetary policy, interest rates will rise in expectation of further depreciation. Suppose, plausibly, that the strong-currency country can refuse to ease. If the economy (or the banking system) in the weak-currency country is fragile enough, the rise in interest rates may convince the central bank to abandon the target zone.

[20] This paragraph draws on Obstfeld and Rogoff (1995, p. 80).

Now suppose a wide band is announced, but that it is initially credible. Again, let fundamentals, not speculators, push the exchange rate to weaken the edge of the band. Because the band is credible, interest rates fall as the currency weakens, in expectation of an appreciation of the exchange rate back to the assumed credible central parity. This fall in interest rates as the economy weakens tends also to reaffirm the initial market view that the regime is credible. This example may imply that a virtuous circle is as possible as a vicious circle. The substantial empirical evidence on this matter, however, suggests that in target-zone systems, interest rates tend to rise toward the edge of the band, not fall, as currencies weaken. A vicious circle cannot therefore be ruled out.[21]

Conducting Monetary Policy When Targeting a (Forward-Looking) Exchange Rate

Kenneth Froot and Maurice Obstfeld (1991) make an important, but insufficiently appreciated, point about the conduct of monetary policy in a credible target-zone system. They show that, even if a target zone is credible, the equilibrium exchange rate is not uniquely defined by a central-bank promise to "do whatever it takes" to preserve the zonal boundaries. In fact, they show that if the central bank can commit only to do whatever it takes, then at each point in time, there are at least three equilibrium exchange rates: an exchange rate consistent with the exogenous fundamentals in the basic model (see Appendix B), an exchange rate that jumps to the weak edge of the band, and an exchange rate that jumps to the strong edge of the band. How can a credible target zone fail to define the exchange rate precisely? It can fail simply because doing "whatever it takes" obligates the central bank to ratify (by means of endogenous jumps in the money supply) self-fulfilling shifts in market expectation. Multiple equilibria under a credible target zone can be ruled out, but this requires that the central bank specify a monetary-policy rule that depends only on exogenous state variables. This is not easy to convey in theory (most of the theoretical literature does not even try). It cannot be any easier to communicate in practice.

Uncertainty Associated with Estimating the Equilibrium Exchange Rate

All of the proposals (save Wolf's [1999]) require an estimate of equilibrium exchange rates to determine the initial central parities and to indicate subsequent adjustments in these parities that are justified by the fundamentals. McKinnon (1997) is firmly of the view that the only

---

[21] Svensson (1992) and Bertola and Caballero (1992) incorporate this evidence into their theory of target zones.

robust basis for this estimate is the PPP for tradable goods. Williamson and Henning (1994) and Williamson (1998) are equally firm in their view that equilibrium nominal exchange rates are those that are consistent with real exchange rates that achieve equilibrium current accounts in the medium term. Thus, the uncertainty associated with estimating the equilibrium exchange rate is not caused only by *parameter* uncertainty, it is also (perhaps primarily) caused by *model* uncertainty. The fundamental equilibrium exchange rates (FEERs) calculated by the IMF and others require estimates of a structural current-account model as well as assumptions about domestic and world saving, investment, and output trends.[22] Exchange rates based on PPP are much easier to calculate but still require deciding how to resolve the base-year problem. The key point is that, given the model uncertainty involved, it is difficult, if not impossible, to know the size of the standard errors associated with an estimate of the equilibrium exchange rate.

Is There a G-3 Exchange-Rate Problem or a Yen Problem?

Figure 6 presents the post-Louvre history of the nominal trade-weighted dollar, the nominal trade-weighted deutsche mark, and the nominal trade-weighted yen. The series are the IMF's nominal effective exchange rates. Also included in each panel are bands at plus and minus 10 percent around the initial 1988 level of the nominal exchange rate. What is apparent is that the considerable variability that is evident in bilateral nominal exchange rates is not present in the nominal trade-weighted dollar or the nominal trade-weighted deutsche mark. The nominal trade-weighted dollar has, since 1988, only rarely and briefly (in 1995 and 1998) departed from a band of plus or minus 10 percent of its 1988 first-quarter level. This is also essentially true for the trade-weighted deutsche mark, which, following unification, strengthened for some time in late 1994 to more than 10 percent of its 1988 level. These three episodes are not difficult to understand. Let us take each in turn.

During 1994 and 1995, the Federal Reserve was concerned that U.S. inflation might rise and pushed up U.S. interest rates in a preemptive strike (Mishkin, 1999; Clarida, Gali, and Gertler, 2000). It does not seem far-fetched to think that, in such a setting, the foreign-exchange market, too, would be concerned about U.S. inflation and that the trade-weighted dollar would weaken. In 1998, by contrast, the U.S. economy was booming, inflation was subdued, and there was a safe-haven flight

---

[22] See Cooper (1994) for a perceptive discussion of the challenges involved in basing exchange-rate policy on FEERs.

FIGURE 6
G-3 NOMINAL EFFECTIVE EXCHANGE RATES SINCE 1988

SOURCE: IMF, *International Financial Statistics*.

to dollar assets. In this environment, it is easy to understand why the trade-weighted dollar strengthened. In Germany, by 1995–96, the Bundesbank was convinced that its earlier tightening in 1990 and 1992 had prevented a ratcheting up of inflation, in part because of the effects of that action on the exchange rate. Faced with a weak economy and strong exchange rate, the Bundesbank eased policy throughout this 1995–96 period of the strong mark.

In Japan, by contrast, the trade-weighted yen has persistently and substantially fluctuated by much more than plus or minus 10 percent of its 1988 level and has closely mimicked the yen-dollar exchange rate. The reason for this is that Japan has considerable trade not only with the United States, but also with countries in Asia that tacitly, if not openly, pegged to the dollar until the onset of the Asia crisis. It is impossible to know how much the yen volatility during the 1990s was driven by fundamentals. Any analysis of this issue must seriously consider market uncertainty about Japanese policies. The newly independent Bank of Japan has not articulated a clear monetary-policy strategy and has found itself in public disputes with the ministry of finance about the appropriate course of monetary policy. In addition, the sheer magnitude of the debt the Japanese government has issued—and will likely continue to issue—has apparently generated significant uncertainty in the global capital markets.

How Much Latitude for National Monetary Policies?

The theory of target zones is clear: if the zone is credible, there can be, especially with wide bands, a great deal of latitude for countries to pursue monetary policies tailored to domestic macroeconomic conditions. Moreover, this latitude does not, under a credible commitment to defend the zonal boundaries, come at the expense of the honeymoon bonus that stabilizes intraband exchange-rate volatility relative to the equilibrium that would prevail in the absence of the zone. However, target-zone theory predicts that the benefit from the honeymoon bonus, even under a credible target zone, is diminished as the width of the band widens, holding constant the extrinsic source of exchange-rate volatility (Appendix B). Thus, even if a wide band is credible, the band itself may do little to diminish intraband exchange-rate volatility. As Svensson (1994a) argues, it appears that the reduction in volatility that is observed in actual target-zone arrangements derives, not from the honeymoon bonus, but in a significant way from a leaning-against-the-wind monetary policy that seeks to keep the exchange rate near the central parity.

Suppose instead, for the reasons outlined above, that the target zone is initially not credible. In this case, the markets expect the same monetary policies that prevailed before the announcement of the zone to continue after the announcement. If this expectation is rational and these policies continue until the exchange rate reaches a zonal boundary, it will be only at this time, and not before, that the markets *can* learn anything about the credibility of the target-zone commitment. Whether or not they *do* learn anything is another matter. As we have just seen, depending on the nature of the shocks hitting the G-3 countries, the monetary policy that is required to meet domestic objectives such as maintaining low inflation and output at potential may also be consistent with reversing an apparent misalignment of the exchange rate relative to the fundamentals. If this is the case as the exchange rate approaches the zonal boundary, the markets will learn nothing about the commitment to the target zone, and no honeymoon bonus can be earned. At some point, however, the zonal boundaries will be approached, and defending them will require that monetary policy be devoted to their defense to the exclusion of domestic objectives. Only at this time will the markets learn something about the target-zone commitment and whether or not the exchange rate is "king." If it is, a honeymoon bonus may begin to be realized, but even after this initial observation, it may take, not just one observation, but several such observations (separated, perhaps, by several years) before the zone has full credibility. Building up credibility for a wide-band target zone may thus take longer, much longer, than might be expected, and the benefits derived from a wide band may be modest (Frankel, 1999, p. 8, makes a similar point).

To appreciate why it might be difficult for the markets to disentangle status quo monetary policy from a commitment to a wide-band target zone, consider the findings of Clarida, Gali, and Gertler (1998), which show that the post-1979 monetary policies of the G-3 are well described by a parsimonious forward-looking Taylor rule of the form

$$R_t = rr + \pi^\circ + \beta \left(\pi^e_{t-1,n} - \pi^\circ \right) + \gamma y_{t-1} \, ,$$

where rr is the equilibrium real interest rate, π° is the (implicit) inflation target, π^e is the expected inflation over the next n periods, and y_{t-1} is the output gap. For example, Clarida, Gali, and Gertler (2000) estimate that $\beta = 2.15$ and $\gamma = 0.93$, using post-1979 quarterly U.S. data. The Clarida-Gali-Gertler framework allows for the central bank to "look at everything" but puts some structure on this old idea by requiring that the weights that the central bank places on the individual pieces of information depend upon the influence this information has on the central bank's inflation forecast. Thus, let $Z_{t-1} = [z_{t-1}, \varepsilon_{t-1}]$ denote an $m + 1$ element vector of lagged information that the central bank uses to forecast inflation, with ε_{t-1} denoting the rate of depreciation of the exchange rate (home-currency price of foreign exchange) relative to its equilibrium level. Suppose that the inflation forecast is a linear function of Z_{t-1}:

$$\pi^e_{t-1,n} - \pi^\circ = \alpha z_{t-1} + \theta \varepsilon_{t-1} .$$

The Clarida-Gali-Gertler forward-looking Taylor rule can, after substitution, be written as

$$R_t = rr + \pi^\circ + \beta\theta\varepsilon_{t-1} + \beta\alpha z_{t-1} + \gamma y_{t-1} .$$

What sort of correlation between the exchange rate and the short-term interest rate would be expected to result from such a status quo monetary policy? This would depend on the sign of θ. Under plausible circumstances, we expect θ to be positive, and there is support for this in the data. This means that when a currency depreciates (relative to, say, PPP), expected inflation tends to rise. The important implication is that, even though a central bank may not target the exchange rate, the bank's desire to stabilize the inflation forecast will lead it to raise nominal and real interest rates when the currency is weakening, and to lower nominal and real interest rates when the currency is strengthening. This reaction will, in turn, tend to strengthen the exchange rate when it is weak and weaken the exchange rate when it is strong (relative to fundamentals). Thus, a monetary policy meant to achieve only domestic objectives may also serve to stabilize the exchange rate.[23] Ironically, this means that it may be more difficult for a central bank that has in the past pursued such a policy to convince the financial markets of its commitment to enforce a wide-band target-zone system.

6   Concluding Remarks

It seems clear that if a G-3 target-zone agreement were put in place under present circumstances, it would initially not be credible. To assume otherwise (and, let us emphasize, the authors of the proposals outlined above do not make this assumption) would be folly in light of the historical record and the challenges that might be faced by any

[23] See Wadhwani, 1999, for an elaboration of this point as it applies to the inflation-targeting strategy of the Bank of England.

such arrangement. The EMS experience reviewed in Appendix A has convinced many serious observers that speculative attacks, even on countries that appeared to be credibly committed to a target zone before the attack, can overwhelm the resolve of governments to make the exchange rate king when there is a conflict between domestic and international objectives.

This conclusion does not mean, however, that over time, a G-3 target zone might not become credible if the G-3 finance ministers and central bankers were committed to it (which they do not at present appear to be, at least in the United States and at the ECB). The IMF's assertion (Goldstein et al., 1993, p. 20), that the exchange rate should always be king is a necessary, but perhaps not a sufficient condition, for credibility. Two aspects of this statement are worth special mention. First, building credibility would take time, perhaps a lot of time. Moreover, as Allan Drazen and Paul Masson (1994) point out, market skepticism about the commitment to the exchange-rate target (zone) might result in speculation against a currency if enforcing the target through tight money were to contribute to a rise in unemployment. Second, the only times that credibility can be "built up" are those times when the internal and external requirements for monetary policy are in conflict. The markets learn nothing about the commitment to a target-zone arrangement when there is no conflict between the monetary policy consistent with domestic objectives and the policy needed to keep the exchange rate inside the band.[24]

The advocates of the proposals for change have assessed the global costs of exchange-rate volatility and of (their estimates of) exchange-rate misalignments, especially as these apply to the emerging economies through their ties to the global capital markets. It is their view that the status quo is unacceptable and that a sustained effort to limit G-3 exchange-rate fluctuations would deliver benefits to the world economy that would outweigh the value of any loss of monetary autonomy in the G-3 that would be required to maintain such a system. The skeptics do not necessarily dispute the benefits to the world economy, but they make a positive, not a normative, judgment that the sorts of proposals that are on the table will not, in practice, get around Krugman's "dilemma of the global financial architecture."

[24] For a discussion of the issues involved with setting exchange-rate policy in EMU, see Kenen (1998a, 1998b); for the United States, see Cross (1998); and for Japan, see Cargill, Hutchison, and Ito (1997).

Appendix A

This appendix reviews the way in which the best-known target-zone arrangement, the exchange-rate mechanism (ERM) of the EMS, operated during the 1990s. The collapse of the original, narrow-band, ERM in 1992–93 made even many of the original EMS supporters (Svensson, 1994b), and certainly most of the skeptics (Obstfeld and Rogoff, 1995), doubtful about the sustainability of a target-zone system in a world of international capital mobility and divergent macroeconomic cycles (caused perhaps in part, but not entirely, by asymmetric shocks). Proponents of the current wide-band proposals for limiting exchange-rate volatility sometimes argue that there is little to learn from the Bundesbank-centered, narrow-band ERM, because the new proposals are designed to avoid the fundamental flaws of the EMS system (see Section 4). The design changes in the new proposals include wider bands and more frequent and systematic adjustment of central parities. The wider bands, which are a feature of all the proposals (if the Wolf proposal is seen as featuring an infinitely wide band with a finite lower support on the euro-dollar and yen-dollar exchange rates), are designed to provide greater leeway for countries to pursue monetary policies that are tailored to local circumstances. The adjustable central parities, which are a feature of the Volcker and Williamson proposals, but not of the McKinnon proposal, are designed to prevent countries from getting into a position of having to defend disequilibrium exchange rates.

Although the motivation for the design changes in these proposals is clear, there is much to be learned from the EMS experience of the 1990s that is relevant to our views about future G-3 exchange-rate arrangements. The ERM, both under the original narrow bands that prevailed until August 1993 and under the wide (plus or minus 15 percent) bands that prevailed afterward, can shed light on the two issues that are central to the present discussion: the degree of monetary autonomy that is actually available in a target-zone system and the extent to which equilibrium exchange rates can become disequilibrium exchange rates as a result of a self-fulfilling speculative run.

Monetary-Policy Autonomy under the ERM: 1990 to 1993

Appendix B states that a credible target zone has an advantage over a fixed exchange rate in that it theoretically allows for a degree of monetary-policy independence in a world of unfettered capital mobility. Under a credible target zone, in which realignment risk is either zero or fluctuates modestly (and independently of the interest differential), a central bank facing a recession at home can drive down short-term interest rates relative to world rates and yet still maintain exchange-rate fluctuations within the target-zone bands. Was this leeway to conduct monetary policy attuned to domestic conditions actually available to the ERM countries? There are reasons to think it was not. Consider, for example, the following from the Bank of England's *Quarterly Bulletin* (1992, p. 7), published just weeks after the September 1992 ERM crisis:

> Against a backdrop of sluggish activity and stable or falling inflation, a number of countries in Europe have experienced a growing conflict between the monetary policy required to maintain the exchange rate, and the policy that would be appropriate given domestic cyclical conditions. In a number of cases, nominal interest rates might have been lower but for the ERM. This was particularly the case for those countries . . . which were . . . in a different cyclical position.

The empirical findings of Clarida, Gali, and Gertler (1998) highlight the extent to which the ERM commitments precluded the member central banks from tailoring their monetary policies to domestic cyclical conditions. In the months leading up to the September 1992 crisis, there was never a month in which the average short-term interest rate in Britain, France, or Italy was driven below the rate prevailing in Germany. Although much of the literature has focused on the fact that these countries' interest differentials with Germany were declining during the period leading up to the crisis (except in Italy where the lira-deutsche mark interest differentials began to rise steeply in August 1992), these interest differentials were always positive. Moreover, Britain and Italy, and to a lesser extent France, were in "different cyclical positions" than Germany was during the months leading up to the crisis. Both Britain and Italy had larger measured output gaps than Germany had, and the gap for France was roughly comparable. Britain's inflation had, by mid-1992, converged to that in Germany; inflation in France was somewhat lower; and inflation in Italy was somewhat higher. These facts suggest that, during an episode in which monetary policy, unfettered by commitments to the ERM, would have been pushing interest rates in Britain, France, and Italy *below* those prevailing in Germany, the ERM commitments (and, in particular, the policies needed to counter the realignment expectations of speculators) forced interest rates in these countries to remain *above* those prevailing in Germany. Thus, under the narrow-band ERM, there was no leeway for countries other than Germany to conduct monetary policies that were in any way attuned to domestic cyclical positions. If any further evidence is required, note that in the days and weeks following the exit of sterling and the lira from the ERM in September 1992, short-term interest rates in Britain and Italy fell sharply.

Clarida, Gali, and Gertler (1998) attempt to quantify the stresses that emerged in Britain, France, and Italy in the months leading up to the ERM crisis. They define $stress_t Britain$ as the difference between the short-term interest rate that prevailed in Britain in month t and the short-term interest rate that would have prevailed had Britain not been committed to the ERM. This "but-for" interest rate is calculated as the rate consistent with a Taylor rule using data on inflation and the estimated output gap for Britain.[25] The authors reach four conclusions. First, in all three countries, the stresses that emerged in the months leading up to the crisis are estimated to have been substantial, roughly 300 basis points in Britain, 500 basis points in France, and 1,000 basis points in Italy—that is, the Clarida-Gali-Gertler stress index indicates that short-term interest rates in Britain at the time of the September 1992 crisis were 300 basis points higher than they would have been (and than they had been just several weeks earlier) without the commitment to remain in the ERM. Second, the magnitude of each of these stress indicators exceeds the leeway for monetary policy under the narrow bands of the ERM that would have been available even in the absence of realignment risk. Third, it is nonetheless still the case that none of these central banks was able or willing to push its interest rates below those in Germany, even though domestic macroeconomic conditions warranted such a move.[26] Fourth, the sources of the stresses that emerged differed from country to country. In Britain, the most important source was the divergence between German and British business cycles; in Italy, it was a sudden adverse shift in market expectations that the lira could remain in the ERM; in France, it was a shift in market sentiment, as well as a tightening of German monetary policy.

The Wide-Band ERM: 1993 to 1998

After August 1993, those countries remaining in the ERM (except for the Netherlands) widened the width of the target zone from plus or

---

[25] The Clarida-Gali-Gertler (1988) forward-looking Taylor rule takes the form $R_t = rr + \pi^* + \beta(\pi^e_{t,n} - \pi^*) + \gamma y_t$, where rr is the equilibrium real interest rate, π^* is the (implicit) inflation target, π^e is expected inflation, and y_t is the output gap.

[26] I do not suggest that these countries were mistaken in trying to maintain their ERM parities, given their revealed preference for exchange-rate stability, but rather that these commitments did, *in practice*, foreclose the option to lower short rates below those in Germany, an option that was, *in theory*, supposed to be available to them. See Kenen (1996) for a useful discussion of this point.

minus 2.5 percent to plus or minus 15 percent. Fluctuation in the franc-deutsche mark exchange rate did not, in fact, approach the wide bands that were permitted after 1993 (although the franc-dollar exchange rate did). Some observers have argued that the ERM experience with wide bands lends credence to the view that such an arrangement is not meaningless but, rather, that by anchoring expectations, it can contribute to exchange-rate stability even if, "most of the time," the bands are not tested. It is clear that something stabilized the franc-deutsche mark exchange rate after August 1993 and that it was not the narrow bands of the original ERM. But was it the "anchoring of expectations" provided by a credible, wide-band ERM? There are several reasons to think it was not.

The very fact that the franc-deutsche mark exchange rate spent most of the time within the original discarded narrow bands of plus or minus 2.5 percent indicates that "France, having been given the leeway for a somewhat weaker franc, chose not to use it" (Krugman, 1997, p. 11). Recall that, in theory, the honeymoon bonus from a target zone derives from the fact that, absent inframarginal interventions, the expectation that the exchange rate cannot wander beyond the (wide) bands stabilizes the exchange rate within these bands. However, if the honeymoon bonus was itself the source of stability in the franc-deutsche mark exchange rate after 1993, the theory would also predict that the exchange rate would have spent "most of the time" near the edges of these wide bands. This was not the case. Rather, it seems clear that after 1993, just as before, French monetary policy was directed toward stabilizing the exchange rate in anticipation of advancing the creation of, and of joining, EMU. This appears to be yet another example of Svensson's (1994a) observation that in practice, if not in theory, successful target-zone systems obligate the central bank to engage in systematic, sustained, and inframarginal nonsterilized intervention operations, in order to keep the exchange rate well within the official bands.[27] It is clear that France did not exploit the freedom it theoretically had to push its interest rates substantially below those in Germany. Indeed, French interest-rate differentials seem to have followed the shifts in realignment expectations.

---

[27] Indeed, Svensson's (1994) model of monetary policy in a target zone specifies a leaning-against-the-wind reaction function for nonsterilized central-bank intervention (monetary policy), which keeps the exchange rate, most of the time, near the central parity. One of the motivations for this reaction function, borne out by the data, is that realignment expectations may be increasing in the deviation from central parity.

What we learn from the wide-band ERM experience of France is that monetary policy, when devoted to a single goal, can maintain the exchange rate within a target zone. We do not learn much about the extent to which the wide-band ERM provided an anchor for expectations or granted leeway to pursue independent monetary policies.

Was the ERM Collapse a Self-Fulfilling Crisis?

In his recent survey paper on currency crises, Krugman (1997, p. 4) outlines the three ingredients that, in retrospect, led to the ERM crisis. First, there was a social cost to staying in the ERM. Britain and Italy, which were faced with "unemployment due to inadequate demand, and with the resulting pressure on monetary authorities to engage in expansionary policies," had reason to abandon the narrow-band ERM, which prevented them from following such policies. Second, there was a political cost to withdrawing from the ERM, perhaps encouraged by the perception *ex ante* that a devaluation would have inflationary consequences. Third, there was an increasing cost to staying in the ERM, in terms of ongoing recession and unemployment, as the markets revised upward their expectation of devaluation, which in turn pushed up short-term interest rates; this was clearly evident in Italy and also, very briefly, in Britain.

These ingredients appear to be present in many recent currency crises. However, they do not necessarily imply that a crisis that results from them is self-fulfilling (Obstfeld and Rogoff, 1995). As Krugman (1997, p. 6) argues:

> It is possible to combine these elements to produce a general story about currency crises that is quite similar to that in the [traditional] model. Suppose that a country's fundamental trade-off between the costs of main-taining the current parity and the costs of abandoning it is predictably deteriorating, so that at some future date the country would be likely to devalue even in the absence of a speculative attack. Then speculators would surely try to get out of the currency ahead of the devaluation—but in so doing they would worsen the government's trade-off, leading to an earlier devaluation. . . . [T]he end result will therefore be a crisis that ends the fixed exchange rate regime well before the fundamentals would appear to make devaluation necessary. . . . [Note that] the crisis is driven by economic fundamentals. Yet, that is not the way it might seem when the crisis actually strikes: the government of the target country would feel that it was fully prepared to maintain the exchange rate for a long time, and would in fact have done so, yet was forced to abandon it by a speculative attack that made defending the rate simply too expensive.

Although the joint presence of the aforementioned three ingredients in the ERM crisis is not sufficient to identify it as self-fulfilling in origin, self-fulfilling crises cannot be ruled out as a matter of theory (Krugman, 1997; Obstfeld and Rogoff, 1997). Suppose, following the argument presented in Krugman (1997), that an eventual end to the target zone is not "preordained." Unemployment in the periphery may be rising because of recession, and banks' balance sheets may be weakening, but so long as short-term interest rates remain at the level set by the center country, the central bank is prepared to "tough it out," perhaps by tolerating disinflation. Now, suppose, for some reason, that the markets sharply revise upward their assessment of a devaluation. This will feed into higher short-term interest rates (and to a lesser extent, long-term interest rates). The central bank now has a more difficult decision to make. Toughing it out when the markets do not expect a central bank to do so may well mean a longer recession, more unemployment, and more bank failures (or rescues) than would otherwise be the case. A "hang-tough" policy that makes sense in the absence of devaluation expectations may very well not be worth the cost when short-term interest rates are pushed up 300, 400, or 500 basis points as a result of arbitrary devaluation expectations. Under certain circumstances, these arbitrary devaluation expectations can become self-fulfilling as the central bank chooses to devalue in the face of a spike in interest rates caused by negative expectations. This argument has been emphasized by Eichengreen, Rose, and Wyplosz (1995, p. 295), who state that

> self-fulfilling attacks rest on a bet by markets that governments will not [sustain] tough policy action. The conditions under which governments hesitate to [maintain] such steps turn out to be obvious: they include recession, high unemployment, past or impending elections, and finance ministers on thin ice. This is why markets are more likely to trigger attacks when a country is in a delicate economic or political situation.

Or, consider the ERM postmortem offered by Svensson (1994b, pp. 456–457), who writes that

> multiple equilibria are possible. In one equilibrium no speculative attack occurs, the exchange rate remains fixed, and monetary policy remains tight. In the other equilibrium a speculative attack occurs, a realignment or free float follows, a monetary policy switches to become more expansionary, *ex post* rationalizing the speculative attack. The Danish "no" and the uncertainty about the French referendum contributed to make the EMU more uncertain and to make [multiple] equilibri[a] more likely. The multiple-equilibria explanation seems relevant for Italy, Britain, and perhaps France.

There is by no means common agreement that the ERM crisis was driven by a self-fulfilling attack; Williamson and Henning (1994) certainly dissent from such an interpretation. Moreover, as Krugman (1997, p. 7) points out, the recent second-generation models of currency crises imply that

> there is a range of fundamentals in which a crisis cannot happen, and a range of fundamentals in which it must happen; at most, self-fulfilling-crisis models say that there is an intermediate range in which a crisis can happen, but need not. . . . Since the logic of predictable crises [driven only by fundamentals] is that they happen well before the fundamentals have reached the point at which the exchange rate would have collapsed in the absence of [an] attack, . . . it will always seem at the time that the crisis has been provoked by a speculative attack not justified by current fundamentals.

Appendix B

The proposals reviewed in this paper share in common a call on the G-3 countries to adopt some form of target-zone system. Because the theoretical case for a target zone was developed originally by Krugman (1991), and because most of the (vast) literature on the subject begins from Krugman's work, his is the model reviewed in this appendix.[28] The original Krugman model, and virtually all its successors, start with the assumption that the exchange rate is a forward-looking asset price that depends on current fundamentals and on expectations about future exchange rates. Holding constant current fundamentals, an exchange rate that is expected to appreciate (depreciate) in the future will also tend to appreciate (depreciate) somewhat today. It is assumed that the (logarithmic) fundamentals are of two types: one that is exogenous to the central bank (denoted as v_t) and one that is under the control of the central bank (denoted as m_t). The (logarithmic) exchange rate is determined according to

$$e_t = m_t + v_t + \alpha E \Delta e_{t+1} .$$

If expectations are rational and bubbles are assumed away,[29] the exchange rate is determined according to a present-value relation by the current level and expected future time path of the composite fundamental

$$k_t = m_t + v_t .^{30}$$

---

[28] The discussion closely follows Svensson's (1992) survey of the subject.
[29] See Frankel (1985) for a discussion of bubbles in the foreign-exchange market.
[30] The solution is $e_t = (1 + \alpha)^{-1} \Sigma_{j=0,\infty} [\alpha/(1 + \alpha)]^j Ek_{t+j}$.

Thus, by controlling the expected future time path of the money supply and, in particular, by allowing the bank to lean against the wind in response to exogenous shocks to v_t, the central bank can, if it chooses, target the exchange rate. Krugman made the very definite assumption about the operation of his target zone that as long as the exchange rate is inside the band, the money supply is constant; the only time that the money supply changes is when the exchange rate moves to the edge of the band, and then only by enough to prevent the exchange rate from moving outside the band in response to a shock to v. Krugman also assumed that increments to v_t are independent, so that the level of v_t is a random walk.

The main finding of the target-zone models is that, under a target zone, the elasticity of the exchange rate with respect to the fundamental is less than one (and, in fact, approaches zero as the exchange rate moves toward the edges of the band). Thus, the exchange rate is less volatile than is the fundamental. Under a free float, by contrast, the exchange rate and the fundamental are equally volatile. This is the famous honeymoon effect, whereby even in the absence of a leaning-against-the-wind monetary policy when the exchange rate is inside the band, the expectation that the central bank will lean against the wind in the future to prevent the exchange rate from drifting outside the band will stabilize the exchange rate in the present. As Svensson (1992, p. 124) puts it: "a target zone means stabilizing the fundamentals . . . but the exchange rate stabilizes even more—some exchange rate stability is for free."

Krugman and Miller (1993) make a different theoretical case for a target zone. They show that if stop-loss trading strategies are prominent in the foreign-exchange market, the exchange rate may be excessively volatile (more volatile than the fundamentals). This is because the rational speculators that remain after the stop-loss traders are gone have anticipated the traders' exit in advance and bid up the price of foreign exchange excessively as the fundamentals have weakened. In such circumstances, a target zone in which the central bank stands ready to sell the foreign currency that is in excess demand when the stop-loss traders exit can stabilize expectations and eliminate the excess volatility of the exchange rate before these traders leave.

One advantage that a credible target zone has as compared to a fixed exchange rate is that the target zone theoretically allows for a degree of monetary independence in a world of unfettered capital mobility (Svensson, 1994a).[31] Indeed, as is argued in Section 5, much of the

[31] The following discussion follows Svensson (1994a), pp. 159–163.

appeal of the proposals for limiting exchange-rate flexibility derives from their promise to relax the constraint imposed by the impossible trinity of international finance. A credible target zone can resolve this conflict by permitting (in theory) a national central bank to adjust, within limits, short-term domestic interest rates in response to domestic macroeconomic conditions, without resorting to capital controls.

To see how this works in theory, let the logarithm of the exchange rate be written as $e_t = c_t + x_t$, where c_t is the central parity and x_t is the deviation from central parity. Uncovered interest parity then implies that

$$R_{t,n} = R_{t,n}^* + E_t \frac{c_{t+n} - c_t}{n} + \frac{E_t(x_{t+n} - x_t)}{n}.$$

Consider, first, the case of a fully credible target zone in which $E_t(c_{t+n} - c_t) = 0$. Suppose, now, that the country is hit with a fall in demand for exports that pushes it into recession. Under a target zone, the central bank can, by engineering a depreciation of the currency, drive down the yield to maturity on an n-year bond by a maximum of χ/n percentage points, where χ is the width of the target zone (relative to central parity) and n is the number of years the markets expect that interest rates will need to stay below world levels in order for the economy to recover from recession and for the central parity to be restored. If n is equal to 3 and χ is equal to 0.1—a value that is often suggested as part of the proposals discussed above—the yield on a one-year bond can be driven down roughly 3.33 percentage points (333 basis points) a year for each of three years, relative to the corresponding yield in the rest of the world. In practice, of course, the instrument of monetary policy is typically a short-term interest rate, whereas in many G-3 countries, it is a longer-term interest rate (say, on a ten-year bond) that influences spending decisions.

Consider, further, the case of a less than fully credible target zone in which expectations of realignment fluctuate. In the simple, and extreme, case in which these fluctuations are entirely random and independent of domestic monetary policy and the real economy, monetary policy still retains a degree of autonomy. A fall in export demand can still be met with a cut in domestic short-term interest rates and an exchange-rate depreciation to the edge of the band. Another source of contraction in domestic demand is introduced by a shift in devaluation expectations. A rise in $E_t c_{t+n}$ puts upward pressure on domestic interest rates (short and long), which, for empirically plausible central-bank reaction functions (such as those estimated by Clarida, Gali, and Gertler, 1998), will encourage the central bank to lean against the wind and stem the rise in domestic interest rates by allowing the exchange rate to depreciate toward (or to) the edge of the band. If both of these events—a contraction in aggregate demand and a (chance) rise in expected devaluation—occur at the same time, the monetary autonomy can be significantly compromised or, indeed, eliminated.

Consider, next, the more realistic case in which fluctuations in expected devaluation depend, at least in part, on the stance of domestic monetary policy and the state of the real economy. To focus attention, consider the hypothesis studied by Svensson (1994a), that $E_t(c_{t+n} - c_t) = \gamma x_t$. According to this specification, the central bank faces a tradeoff. If it meets a fall in aggregate demand with a temporary depreciation of the exchange rate to the edge of the band, this effort to lower the domestic interest rate will be frustrated by the upward revision in devaluation expectations that depreciation causes. In particular,

$$R_{t,n} = R_{t,n}^* + E_t \frac{x_{t+n} - (1 - \gamma)x_t}{n}.$$

Consider, as does Svensson (1994a), the case in which $\gamma = 0.7$. Continuing with the earlier example in which n is equal to 3 and χ is equal to 0.1 when $\gamma = 0.7$, the yield on a one-year bond can be driven down by only 1 percentage point (100 basis points) a year for each of three years, relative to the corresponding yield in the rest of the world, and the ten-year yield can be driven down by only 30 basis points.

References

Bank of England, *Quarterly Bulletin*, London, Bank of England, November 1992.

Bertola, Giuseppe, and Ricardo J. Caballero, "Target Zones and Realignments," *American Economic Review*, 82 (June 1992), pp. 520–536.

Beveridge, Stephen, and Charles Nelson, "A New Approach to Decomposition of Economic Time Series into Permanent and Transitory Components with Particular Attention to Measurement of the 'Business Cycle,'" *Journal of Monetary Economics*, 7 (March 1981), pp. 151–174.

Bhagwati, Jagdish, "Yes to Free Trade, Maybe to Capital Controls," *Wall Street Journal*, November 16, 1998.

Calomiris, Charles, "Blueprints for a New Global Financial Architecture," Graduate School of Business, Columbia University, October 1998, processed.

Campa, José Manuel, and Linda S. Goldberg, "Investment, Pass-Through, and Exchange Rates: A Cross-Country Comparison," *International Economic Review*, 40 (May 1999), pp. 287–314.

Cargill, Thomas F., Michael M. Hutchison, and Takatoshi Ito, *The Political Economy of Japanese Monetary Policy*, Cambridge, Mass., and London, MIT Press, 1997.

Catte, Pietro, Giampaolo Galli, and Salvatore Rebecchini, "Exchange Markets Can Be Managed!" *International Economic Insights* (September 1992), pp. 17–21.

Clarida, Richard H., and Jordi Gali, "Sources of Real Exchange-Rate Fluctuations: How Important Are Nominal Shocks?" *Carnegie-Rochester Conference Series on Public Policy*, 41 (December 1994), pp. 1–56.

Clarida, Richard H., Jordi Gali, and Mark Gertler, "Monetary Policy Rules in Practice: Some International Evidence," *European Economic Review*, 42 (June 1998), pp. 1033–1067.

————, "The Science of Monetary Policy: A New Keynesian Perspective," *Journal of Economic Literature*, 37 (December 1999), pp. 1661–1707.

————, "Monetary Policy Rules and Macroeconomic Stability: Evidence and Some Theory," *Quarterly Journal of Economics*, 115 (February 2000), pp. 147–181.

Clarida, Richard H., and Mark Gertler, "How the Bundesbank Conducts Monetary Policy," in Christina D. Romer and David H. Romer, eds., *Reducing Inflation: Motivation and Strategy*, Chicago, University of Chicago Press, 1997.

Cooper, Richard N., "Comment on Williamson and Henning," in Peter B. Kenen, ed., *Managing the World Economy: Fifty Years After Bretton Woods*, Washington, D.C., Institute for International Economics, 1994, pp. 112–116.

Cross, Sam, *All About the Foreign Exchange Market in the United States*, New York, Federal Reserve Bank of New York, 1998.

Cumby, Robert E., and John Huizinga, "The Predictability of Real Exchange Rate Changes in the Short and Long Run," National Bureau of Economic Research Working Paper No. 3468, Cambridge, Mass., National Bureau of Economic Research, October 1990.

Drazen, Allan, and Paul R. Masson, "Credibility of Policies Versus Credibility of Policymakers," *Quarterly Journal of Economics*, 109 (August 1994), pp. 735–754.

Dominguez, Kathryn M., and Jeffrey A. Frankel, *Does Foreign Exchange Intervention Work?* Washington, D.C., Institute for International Economics, 1993.

Dornbusch, Rudiger, "Expectations and Exchange Rate Dynamics," *Journal of Political Economy*, 84 (December 1976), pp. 1161–1176; reprinted in Ronald MacDonald and Mark P. Taylor, eds., *Exchange-Rate Economics. Volume 1*, International Library of Critical Writings in Economics, vol. 16, Aldershot, Elgar, 1992, pp. 217–232.

————, "After Asia: New Directions for the International Financial System," *Journal of Policy Modeling*, 21 (May 1999), pp. 289–299.

Edison, Hali J., *The Effectiveness of Central-Bank Intervention: A Survey of the Literature After 1982*, Special Papers in International Economics No. 18, Princeton, N.J., Princeton University, International Finance Section, July 1993.

Eichenbaum, Martin, and Charles Evans, "Some Empirical Evidence on the Effects of Monetary Policy Shocks on Real Exchange Rates," *Quarterly Journal of Economics*, 110 (November 1995), pp. 975–1009.

Eichengreen, Barry, *Towards a New International Financial Architecture*, Washington, D.C., Institute for International Economics, 1999.

Eichengreen, Barry, and Peter B. Kenen, "Managing the World Economy Under the Bretton Woods System," in Peter B. Kenen, ed., *Managing the World Economy: Fifty Years After Bretton Woods*, Washington, D.C., Institute for International Economics, 1994, pp. 3–57.

Eichengreen, Barry, Andrew K. Rose, and Charles Wyplosz, "Exchange Market Mayhem: The Antecedents and Aftermath of Speculative Attacks," *Economic Policy: A European Forum*, 21 (October 1995), pp. 249–296.

Feldstein, Martin, "Self Protection for Emerging Market Economies," National Bureau of Economic Research Working Paper No. 6907, Cambridge, Mass., National Bureau of Economic Research, January 1999.

Frankel, Jeffrey A., "The Dazzling Dollar," *Brookings Papers on Economic Activity*, No. 1 (1985), pp. 199–217.

———, *No Single Currency Regime is Right for All Countries or All Times*, Essays in International Finance No. 215, Princeton, N.J., Princeton University, International Finance Section, August 1999.

Frankel, Jeffrey A., and Andrew K. Rose, "A Panel Project on Purchasing Power Parity: Mean Reversion within and between Countries," *Journal of International Economics*, 40 (February 1996), pp. 209–224.

Froot, Kenneth A., and Maurice Obstfeld, "Exchange Rate Dynamics Under Stochastic Regime Shifts: A Unified Approach," *Journal of International Economics*, 31 (November 1991), pp. 203–229.

Goldberg, Linda S., and Charles D. Kolstad, "Foreign Direct Investment, Exchange Rate Variability, and Demand Uncertainty," *International Economic Review*, 36 (November 1995), pp. 855–873.

Goldstein, Morris, David Folkerts-Landau, Peter M. Garber, Liliana Rojas-Suárez, and Michael G. Spencer, *International Capital Markets, Part I. Exchange Rate Management and International Capital Flows*, Washington D.C., International Monetary Fund, April 1993.

Henderson, Dale W., and Stephanie Sampson, "Intervention in Foreign Exchange Markets: A Summary of Ten Staff Studies," *Federal Reserve Bulletin*, Washington, D.C., Board of Governors of the Federal Reserve System, November 1983, pp. 830–836.

International Monetary Fund (IMF), *International Financial Statistics*, Washington, D.C., International Monetary Fund, various years.

Kenen, Peter B., *Sorting Out Some EMU Issues*, Princeton Reprints in International Finance No. 29, Princeton, N.J., Princeton University, International Finance Section, December 1996.

———, "EMU and Transatlantic Economic Relations," HWWA Discussion Paper No. 60, Hamburg, HWWA-Institut für Wirtschaftsforschung-Hamburg, May 1998a.

———, "Monetary Policy in Stage Three: A Review of the Framework Proposed by the European Monetary Institute," *International Journal of Finance and Economics*, 3 (January 1998b), pp. 3–12.

Kenen, Peter B., and Dani Rodrik, "Measuring and Analyzing the Effects of Short Term Volatility in Real Exchange Rates," *Review of Economics and*

Statistics, 68 (May 1986), pp. 311–315; reprinted in Kenen, *Exchange Rates and the Monetary System: Selected Essays of Peter B. Kenen*, Economists of the Twentieth Century Series, Aldershot, Elgar, 1994, pp. 348–352.

Krugman, Paul R., "Target Zones and Exchange Rate Dynamics," *Quarterly Journal of Economics*, 106 (August 1991), pp. 669–682.

———, "Currency Crises," Department of Economics, Massachusetts Institute of Technology, 1997, processed.

———, "The Euro: Beware of What You Wish For," Department of Economics, Massachusetts Institute of Technology, 1998a, processed.

———, "The Eternal Triangle," Department of Economics, Massachusetts Institute of Technology, 1998b, processed.

Krugman, Paul R., and Marcus H. Miller, "Why Have a Target Zone?" *Carnegie-Rochester Conference Series on Public Policy*, 38 (June 1993), pp. 279–314.

McKinnon, Ronald I., *The Rules of the Game*, Cambridge, Mass., MIT Press, 1997.

———, "International Money: Dollars, Euros, or Yen?" Department of Economics, Stanford University, 1998, processed.

McKinnon, Ronald I., and Kenichi Ohno, *Dollar and Yen*, Cambridge, Mass., MIT Press, 1997.

Mark, Nelson C., "Exchange Rates and Fundamentals: Evidence on Long-Horizon Predictability," *American Economic Review*, 85 (March 1995), pp. 201–218.

Mishkin, Frederic S., "International Experiences with Different Monetary Policy Regimes," National Bureau of Economic Research Working Paper No. 7044, Cambridge, Mass., National Bureau of Economic Research, March 1999.

Mussa, Michael L., "A Model of Exchange Rate Dynamics," *Journal of Political Economy*, February 1982, pp. 74–104.

Obstfeld, Maurice, "International Currency Experience," *Brookings Papers on Economic Activity*, No. 1 (1995), pp. 119–196.

———, "The Global Capital Market: Benefactor or Menace?" *Journal of Economic Perspectives*, 12 (Fall 1998), pp. 9–30.

Obstfeld, Maurice, and Kenneth S. Rogoff, "The Mirage of Fixed Exchange Rates," *Journal of Economic Perspectives*, 9 (Fall 1995), pp. 73–96.

———, *Foundations of International Macroeconomics*, Cambridge, Mass., MIT Press, 1997.

Organisation for Economic Co-operation and Development (OECD), *Main Economic Indicators*, Paris, Organisation for Economic Co-operation and Development, various years.

Prendergast, Joe, "Global Foreign Exchange Research and Strategy," New York, Credit Suisse First Boston, October 1997, processed.

Svensson, Lars E. O., "An Interpretation of Recent Research on Exchange Rate Target Zones," *Journal of Economic Perspectives*, 6 (Fall 1992), pp. 119–144.

———, "Why Exchange Rate Bands? Monetary Independence in Spite of Fixed Exchange Rates." *Journal of Monetary Economics*, 33 (February 1994a), pp. 157–199.

———, "Fixed Exchange Rates as a Means to Price Stability: What Have We Learned?" *European Economic Review*, 38 (April 1994b), pp. 447–468.

Volcker, Paul A., "The Quest for Exchange Rate Stability," Washington, D.C., Institute for International Economics, 1995, processed.

Wadhwani, Sushil B., "Currency Puzzles," London, Bank of England, September 1999, processed.

Williamson, John, "Target Zones and the Management of the Dollar," *Brookings Papers on Economic Activity*, No. 1 (1986), pp. 165–174.

———, *Estimating Equilibrium Exchange Rates*, Washington, D.C., Institute for International Economics, 1994.

———, "Crawling Bands or Monitoring Bands," *International Finance*, 1 (1998), pp. 1–24.

Williamson, John, and Randall C. Henning, "Managing the Monetary System," in Peter B. Kenen, ed., *Managing the World Economy: Fifty Years After Bretton Woods*, Washington, D.C., Institute for International Economics, 1994, pp. 83–111

Wolf, Martin, "Off Target," *Financial Times*, January 30, 1999, p. 11.

PUBLICATIONS OF THE
INTERNATIONAL ECONOMICS SECTION

Notice to Contributors

The International Economics Section publishes papers in two series. ESSAYS IN INTERNATIONAL ECONOMICS and PRINCETON STUDIES IN INTERNATIONAL ECONOMICS. Two earlier series, REPRINTS IN INTERNATIONAL ECONOMICS and SPECIAL PAPERS IN INTERNATIONAL ECONOMICS, have been discontinued, with the SPECIAL PAPERS being absorbed into the STUDIES series.

The Section welcomes the submission of manuscripts focused on topics in international trade, international macroeconomics, or international finance. Submissions should address systemic issues for the global economy or, if concentrating on particular economies, should adopt a comparative perspective.

ESSAYS IN INTERNATIONAL ECONOMICS are meant to disseminate new views about international economic events and policy issues. They should be accessible to a broad audience of professional economists.

PRINCETON STUDIES IN INTERNATIONAL ECONOMICS are devoted to new research in international economics or to synthetic treatments of a body of literature. They should be comparable in originality and technical proficiency to papers published in leading economic journals. Papers that are longer and more complete than those publishable in the professional journals are welcome.

Manuscripts should be submitted in triplicate, typed single sided and double spaced throughout on 8½ by 11 white bond paper. Publication can be expedited if manuscripts are computer keyboarded in WordPerfect or a compatible program. Additional instructions and a style guide are available from the Section or on the website at www.princeton.edu/~ies.

How to Obtain Publications

The Section's publications are distributed free of charge to college, university, and public libraries and to nongovernmental, nonprofit research institutions. Eligible institutions may ask to be placed on the Section's permanent mailing list.

Individuals and institutions not qualifying for free distribution may receive all publications for the calendar year for a subscription fee of $45.00. Late subscribers will receive all back issues for the year during which they subscribe.

Publications may be ordered individually, with payment made in advance. ESSAYS and REPRINTS cost $10.00 each; STUDIES and SPECIAL PAPERS cost $13.50. An additional $1.50 should be sent for postage and handling within the United States, Canada, and Mexico; $2.25 should be added for surface delivery outside the region.

All payments must be made in U.S. dollars. Subscription fees and charges for single issues will be waived for organizations and individuals in countries where foreign-exchange regulations prohibit dollar payments.

Information about the Section and its publishing program is available on the Section's website at www.princeton.edu/~ies. A subscription and order form is printed at the end of this volume. Correspondence should be addressed to:

International Economics Section
Department of Economics, Fisher Hall
Princeton University
Princeton, New Jersey 08544-1021
Tel: 609-258-4048 • Fax: 609-258-1374
E-mail: ies@princeton.edu

List of Recent Publications

A complete list of publications is available at the International Economics Section website at www.princeton.edu/~ies.

ESSAYS IN INTERNATIONAL ECONOMICS
(formerly Essays in International Finance)

180. Warren L. Coats, Jr., Reinhard W. Furstenberg, and Peter Isard, *The SDR System and the Issue of Resource Transfers*. (December 1990)
181. George S. Tavlas, *On the International Use of Currencies: The Case of the Deutsche Mark*. (March 1991)
182. Tommaso Padoa-Schioppa, ed., with Michael Emerson, Kumiharu Shigehara, and Richard Portes, *Europe After 1992: Three Essays*. (May 1991)
183. Michael Bruno, *High Inflation and the Nominal Anchors of an Open Economy*. (June 1991)
184. Jacques J. Polak, *The Changing Nature of IMF Conditionality*. (September 1991)
185. Ethan B. Kapstein, *Supervising International Banks: Origins and Implications of the Basle Accord*. (December 1991)
186. Alessandro Giustiniani, Francesco Papadia, and Daniela Porciani, *Growth and Catch-Up in Central and Eastern Europe: Macroeconomic Effects on Western Countries*. (April 1992)
187. Michele Fratianni, Jürgen von Hagen, and Christopher Waller, *The Maastricht Way to EMU*. (June 1992)
188. Pierre-Richard Agénor, *Parallel Currency Markets in Developing Countries: Theory, Evidence, and Policy Implications*. (November 1992)
189. Beatriz Armendariz de Aghion and John Williamson, *The G-7's Joint-and-Several Blunder*. (April 1993)
190. Paul Krugman, *What Do We Need to Know about the International Monetary System?* (July 1993)
191. Peter M. Garber and Michael G. Spencer, *The Dissolution of the Austro-Hungarian Empire: Lessons for Currency Reform*. (February 1994)
192. Raymond F. Mikesell, *The Bretton Woods Debates: A Memoir*. (March 1994)
193. Graham Bird, *Economic Assistance to Low-Income Countries: Should the Link be Resurrected?* (July 1994)
194. Lorenzo Bini-Smaghi, Tommaso Padoa-Schioppa, and Francesco Papadia, *The Transition to EMU in the Maastricht Treaty*. (November 1994)
195. Ariel Buira, *Reflections on the International Monetary System*. (January 1995)
196. Shinji Takagi, *From Recipient to Donor: Japan's Official Aid Flows, 1945 to 1990 and Beyond*. (March 1995)
197. Patrick Conway, *Currency Proliferation: The Monetary Legacy of the Soviet Union*. (June 1995)
198. Barry Eichengreen, *A More Perfect Union? The Logic of Economic Integration*. (June 1996)
199. Peter B. Kenen, ed., with John Arrowsmith, Paul De Grauwe, Charles A. E. Goodhart, Daniel Gros, Luigi Spaventa, and Niels Thygesen, *Making EMU Happen—Problems and Proposals: A Symposium*. (August 1996)

200. Peter B. Kenen, ed., with Lawrence H. Summers, William R. Cline, Barry Eichengreen, Richard Portes, Arminio Fraga, and Morris Goldstein, *From Halifax to Lyons: What Has Been Done about Crisis Management?* (October 1996)
201. Louis W. Pauly, *The League of Nations and the Foreshadowing of the International Monetary Fund.* (December 1996)
202. Harold James, *Monetary and Fiscal Unification in Nineteenth-Century Germany: What Can Kohl Learn from Bismarck?* (March 1997)
203. Andrew Crockett, *The Theory and Practice of Financial Stability.* (April 1997)
204. Benjamin J. Cohen, *The Financial Support Fund of the OECD: A Failed Initiative.* (June 1997)
205. Robert N. McCauley, *The Euro and the Dollar.* (November 1997)
206. Thomas Laubach and Adam S. Posen, *Disciplined Discretion: Monetary Targeting in Germany and Switzerland.* (December 1997)
207. Stanley Fischer, Richard N. Cooper, Rudiger Dornbusch, Peter M. Garber, Carlos Massad, Jacques J. Polak, Dani Rodrik, and Savak S. Tarapore, *Should the IMF Pursue Capital-Account Convertibility?* (May 1998)
208. Charles P. Kindleberger, *Economic and Financial Crises and Transformations in Sixteenth-Century Europe.* (June 1998)
209. Maurice Obstfeld, *EMU: Ready or Not?* (July 1998)
210. Wilfred Ethier, *The International Commercial System.* (September 1998)
211. John Williamson and Molly Mahar, *A Survey of Financial Liberalization.* (November 1998)
212. Ariel Buira, *An Alternative Approach to Financial Crises.* (February 1999)
213. Barry Eichengreen, Paul Masson, Miguel Savastano, and Sunil Sharma, *Transition Strategies and Nominal Anchors on the Road to Greater Exchange-Rate Flexibility.* (April 1999)
214. Curzio Giannini, *"Enemy of None but a Common Friend of All"? An International Perspective on the Lender-of-Last-Resort Function.* (June 1999)
215. Jeffrey A. Frankel, *No Single Currency Regime Is Right for All Countries or at All Times.* (August 1999)
216. Jacques J. Polak, *Streamlining the Financial Structure of the International Monetary Fund.* (September 1999)
217. Gustavo H. B. Franco, *The Real Plan and the Exchange Rate.* (April 2000)
218. Thomas D. Willett, *International Financial Markets as Sources of Crises or Discipline: The Too Much, Too Late Hypothesis.* (May 2000)
219. Richard H. Clarida, *G-3 Exchange-Rate Relationships: A Review of the Record and of Proposals for Change.* (September 2000)

PRINCETON STUDIES IN INTERNATIONAL ECONOMICS
(formerly Princeton Studies in International Finance)

69. Felipe Larraín and Andrés Velasco, *Can Swaps Solve the Debt Crisis? Lessons from the Chilean Experience.* (November 1990)
70. Kaushik Basu, *The International Debt Problem, Credit Rationing and Loan Pushing: Theory and Experience.* (October 1991)
71. Daniel Gros and Alfred Steinherr, *Economic Reform in the Soviet Union: Pas de Deux*

between Disintegration and Macroeconomic Destabilization. (November 1991)

72. George M. von Furstenberg and Joseph P. Daniels, *Economic Summit Declarations, 1975-1989: Examining the Written Record of International Cooperation.* (February 1992)
73. Ishac Diwan and Dani Rodrik, *External Debt, Adjustment, and Burden Sharing: A Unified Framework.* (November 1992)
74. Barry Eichengreen, *Should the Maastricht Treaty Be Saved?* (December 1992)
75. Adam Klug, *The German Buybacks, 1932-1939: A Cure for Overhang?* (November 1993)
76. Tamim Bayoumi and Barry Eichengreen, *One Money or Many? Analyzing the Prospects for Monetary Unification in Various Parts of the World.* (September 1994)
77. Edward E. Leamer, *The Heckscher-Ohlin Model in Theory and Practice.* (February 1995)
78. Thorvaldur Gylfason, *The Macroeconomics of European Agriculture.* (May 1995)
79. Angus S. Deaton and Ronald I. Miller, *International Commodity Prices, Macroeconomic Performance, and Politics in Sub-Saharan Africa.* (December 1995)
80. Chander Kant, *Foreign Direct Investment and Capital Flight.* (April 1996)
81. Gian Maria Milesi-Ferretti and Assaf Razin, *Current-Account Sustainability.* (October 1996)
82. Pierre-Richard Agénor, *Capital-Market Imperfections and the Macroeconomic Dynamics of Small Indebted Economies.* (June 1997)
83. Michael Bowe and James W. Dean, *Has the Market Solved the Sovereign-Debt Crisis?* (August 1997)
84. Willem H. Buiter, Giancarlo M. Corsetti, and Paolo A. Pesenti, *Interpreting the ERM Crisis: Country-Specific and Systemic Issues.* (March 1998)
85. Holger C. Wolf, *Transition Strategies: Choices and Outcomes.* (June 1999)
86. Alessandro Prati and Garry J. Schinasi, *Financial Stability in European Economic and Monetary Union.* (August 1999)
87. Peter Hooper, Karen Johnson, and Jaime Marquez, *Trade Elasticities for the G-7 Countries.* (August 2000)

SPECIAL PAPERS IN INTERNATIONAL ECONOMICS

17. Richard Pomfret, *International Trade Policy with Imperfect Competition.* (August 1992)
18. Hali J. Edison, *The Effectiveness of Central-Bank Intervention: A Survey of the Literature After 1982.* (July 1993)
19. Sylvester W.C. Eijffinger and Jakob De Haan, *The Political Economy of Central-Bank Independence.* (May 1996)
20. Olivier Jeanne, *Currency Crises: A Perspective on Recent Theoretical Developments.* (March 2000)

REPRINTS IN INTERNATIONAL ECONOMICS
(formerly Reprints in International Finance)

29. Peter B. Kenen, *Sorting Out Some EMU Issues*; reprinted from Jean Monnet Chair Paper 38, Robert Schuman Centre, European University Institute, 1996. (December 1996)

56

fold over, seal, and send

° SUBSCRIBE ° ORDER °

INTERNATIONAL ECONOMICS SECTION

SUBSCRIPTIONS

Rate $45 a year

The International Economics Section issues six to eight publications each year in a mix of Essays, Studies, and occasional Reprints. Late subscribers receive all publications for the subscription year. Prepayment is required and may be made by check in U.S. dollars or by Visa or MasterCard. A complete list of publications is available at www.princeton.edu/~ies.

Address inquiries to:

International Economics Section
Department of Economics, Fisher Hall
Princeton University
Princeton, NJ 08544–1021

BOOK ORDERS

Essays & Reprints	$10.00
Studies & Special Papers	$13.50

plus postage

Within U.S.	$1.50
Outside U.S. (surface mail)	$2.25

_____

Discounts are available for book dealers and for orders of five or more publications.

_____

Telephone: 609–258–4048
Telefax: 609–258–1374
E-mail: ies@princeton.edu

fold up

INTERNATIONAL ECONOMICS SECTION

This is a subscription ☐ ; a book order ☐

Essay #(s) _____, _____ No. of copies___

Study #(s) _____, _____ No. of copies___

Special Paper # _____ No. of copies___

Reprint # _____ No. of copies___

☐ Enclosed is my check made payable to Princeton University, International Economics Section

totaling $_____.

Please charge: ☐ Visa ☐ MasterCard

Acct.# _____

Expires _____

Signature_____

Send to:

Name_____

Address_____

City _____

State _____Zip _____

Country_____

INTERNATIONAL ECONOMICS SECTION
DEPARTMENT OF ECONOMICS
FISHER HALL
PRINCETON UNIVERSITY
PRINCETON, NJ 08544-1021